Into a

WILD SANCTUARY

Into a

WILD SANCTUARY

A Life in Music & Natural Sound

Bernie Krause
Introduction by Jack Turner

Heyday Books
Berkeley, California

Portions of the text are reprinted with permission from *Notes From the Wild* (Ellipsis Arts, 1996)

Library of Congress Cataloging-in-Publication Data:

Krause, Bernard L.
    Into a wild sanctuary : a life in music and natural sound / by Bernie Krause ; introduction by Jack Turner.
        p.   cm.
        ISBN 1-890771-15-5 (cloth). — ISBN 1-890771-11-2 (pbk.)
        1. Krause, Bernard L. 2. Musicians—United States-Biography. 3. Nature sounds—Recording and reproducing. I. Title.
    ML419.K74A3 1998
    780'.92—dc21
    [B]
                                        98-29177
                                           CIP
                                         MN

Cover Image: © 1997, PhotoDisc, Inc.
Cover Design: Jack Myers, Design Site, Berkeley, California
Interior Design/Typesetting: Rebecca LeGates
Editing: Julianna Fleming
Editorial Assistant: Simone Scott
Printing and Binding: Publishers Press, Salt Lake City

Orders, inquiries, and correspondence should be addressed to:
Heyday Books
P. O. Box 9145, Berkeley, CA 94709
510/549-3564, Fax 510/549-1889
heyday@heydaybooks.com

Printed in the United States of America

10 9 8 7 6 5 4 3 2 1

To Ken Norris, the guide ever strong and tactful, full of life and good humor, who taught me to hear the music of the natural world in ways I would have never otherwise discovered, and who has patiently led so many of us to discover its endless marvels. Woof, to you.

Contents

Part II

(chapter titles from Song of Myself *by Walt Whitman)*

Introduction

Into a Wild Sanctuary is an autobiography, mostly an intellectual autobiography, that records the highlights of a life devoted to sounds and to music. Because it covers so much ground, personal and cultural, it will appeal to different readers for widely different reasons. But for me it is especially interesting because of the author's radical notions about "acoustical ecology," a field that came into existence only in the late 1970s, for which his research and speculations will, I have no doubt, serve as prolegomena.

Bernie Krause is both a musician and a naturalist, and a genius in both areas. During the fifties and sixties, he devoted himself to music—jazz, pop, blues, folk, and even gospel—with more success than he seems willing to give himself credit for. But it wasn't until 1965, when he was introduced to electronic music by Karlheinz Stockhausen, that he broke with our conventional musical heritage. His new interest led him to the Moog synthesizer, of which he was an early champion, and after that, nearly everything Krause has done in the world of music and sound has been marked by the idea of synthesis.

Krause has approached the richness of natural soundscapes as both a musician and a naturalist. As a naturalist—Krause has a doctorate and wrote a thesis on bio-acoustics—he has recorded soundscapes throughout the world. Obtaining adequate data for a single site typically requires 500 hours of field recording to get fifteen minutes of usable material, making Krause's understanding of different habitats even more impressive; the intensive labor involved in gathering data also reveals the diversity within restricted sections of habitats, a complexity to which we are, literally, deaf. His collection of environmental sound, the largest private collection in the world, contains 3,500 hours of entire habitats—20 percent of which are now extinct.

Krause realized that the natural soundscapes he recorded might also be used as music, even altered with a synthesizer. Here the artist/conductor plays with natural sounds the way a painter plays with color, transforming reality into a unique composition. It is not possible to convey in words the impact of Krause's recordings, many of which are available through his own label, Wild Sanctuary, distributed by Miramar Recordings. I love the sound of sand dunes singing as they shift, the movement of water in the phloem of a tree, the astounding gong-like call of a male walrus.

Of particular concern to Krause is what he calls the "profound breach" created by the loss, in the West, of the relationship between music and natural sounds. While investigating this subject, he became increasingly aware of our ignorance of nature's aural dimension in a culture dominated by visual experience. Even when we do direct our attention to natural sound, it is always to individual sounds—a bird's song, thunder, an insect's buzz. We do not attend to the synthesis of these sounds. Instead of a cacophony, a natural soundscape can be seen as a symphony, a spontaneous composition with structure, with each individual creature occupying the position of a particular instrument or voice in a coherent whole. People from some remaining traditional cultures, Krause discovered, possess the acuity not only to respond to individual sounds within this aural complexity, but to perceive its overall structure and even to build upon it with their own compositions. Western Civilization must now consider wholly new possibilities for making music, perhaps even for communication, with older and more complex cultures.

For me, one of the most intoxicating aspects of Krause's long odyssey is his discovery of biophony—"the combined sound that whole groups of living organisms produce in any given biome." As Gary Snyder has pointed out, human language is wild—organizing and reorganizing itself independently of human will. Krause suggests that the communicative structures of a biome are also wild—a constantly changing, reflexive synthesis of sound.

Among his greatest contributions to our understanding of the world is his identification of "acoustical niches," the ways in which different species within a single soundscape jostle for acoustical territory and unoccupied frequencies in which they can communicate. By recognizing acoustical niches, something creative and important emerges: the possibility (I believe the reality) that acoustical ecology is as important as spatial ecology, with communication as significant in defining territory, habitat, and ecological integrity as, say, trophic structure. Territory, habitat, and ecological integrity may now no longer be definable in the three spatial dimensions alone. We need to add sound as a fourth dimension. And since some traditional people can tell where they are by smell, and smells and secretions vary with species, our concept of habitat may require five dimensions—or more. Which, at the very least, suggests we should consider our impacts on environments with even greater humility.

With our proclivity for visual definition, we tend to describe wildness through its spatial dimension. Krause's focus on the aural expands our sense of the wild by, literally, expanding the boundaries of perception. It also rivets us to the present tense—to life as it is— singing in its full-throated ease. No doubt each singer is striving for survival, but also is part of an ever-changing, complex whole that Krause's work allows us to enter, as if for the first time. Krause takes us into a wilder world beyond the mundane and the merely visual, suggesting, as the insights of all great naturalists have, that wild nature is both more complex and more compelling than meets the eye.

Jack Turner
July 1998

BIOPHANY—n. an insight about the natural world of living organisms as we allow it to be revealed to us. A particular vision or appearance of biological life.

BIOPHONY—n. the combined sound that whole groups of living organisms produce in any given biome.

Prologue

Karisoke (Rwanda). Dian Fossey's camp

It was my second day in the field recording sounds at this remote site. At first, everything went smoothly. The researchers and guides, reassured that I could be left alone with my gear, went off to document their own observations. Settling down to work, I didn't notice that I had inadvertently positioned myself between Pablo, a young male silverback mountain gorilla, and Ziz, the dominant male. Pablo, who sat sulking away from the other gorillas, had been caught trying to mate with one of Ziz's favorite females and had subsequently been pounced on by the alpha beast. My recorder was running and I was sitting with my back to Pablo when I heard an explosive crash. With stereo microphones, it was impossible to tell that the crash I heard was coming from directly behind me. It was only when Pablo's large, hairy, black hand grabbed my right shoulder, picked me up, equipment and all, and flung me fifteen feet through the air that I learned the painful truth. But other than the incredible smarting pain on the side of my face when I landed in a patch of stinging nettles, I escaped major injury.

Antarctic

As I sat on a rock outcrop in a well-padded dry suit, I saw at least two or three hundred killer whales (*Orcinus orca*) milling about at the surface. The sea was calm, and it was my first really good sound recording opportunity in two weeks at this site. One magnificent male orca with a seven- or eight-foot dorsal fin had been spy-hopping (thrusting his head vertically out of the water to look around) for fifteen minutes directly in front of me. He swam closer to where I was perched and lunged upward—holding a vertical position for an unusual length of time before finally settling into the water. Instinctively, I reached for my recorder and clutched it tightly. Then, not ten feet away from where I sat, the whale suddenly leapt out of the water *onto the ledge* and snaked his way onto the rock shelf. I hadn't noticed the Emperor penguins grouped inland behind me—but he had. Moving swiftly on his belly, the whale chased the birds over the rocks until he caught one. Then, with great agility, he turned around with bird in mouth, slithered to the ledge, and slipped back into the water with his well-earned meal.

The North Slope in Alaska, seventy-five miles east of Barrow near Pitt Point on the Beaufort Sea

I had pitched my tent here for ten days. I was alone with a few good books, just the way I like it. It was late spring, and the ice was beginning to break up; the lengthening daylight made things easier although it was still chilly, -20°F. A few distant recordings of whales and the marvelous glissandos of bearded seals (which sound like missiles falling in a World War II movie) were finally on tape. While warming up the twelve recorder batteries under my arm that morning, I heard a crunching noise on the ice at the back of my tent. Odd, I thought. I hadn't heard a plane land or anyone approach. Perhaps it was a seal or a large bird. Or maybe I was afloat on an ice flow.

Still in my thermal underwear, I unzipped the tent flap and peered outside to find a polar bear standing less than twenty feet away, sniffing the air and looking in my direction, its massive off-white head slowly oscillating back and forth as if deciding what to do next. Cautiously, I moved back into the tent, reaching for my only semblance of a weapon—a flare gun. Quickly slipping on my boots, I cocked the gun, stepped outside, and waited to see if the animal would move a bit closer. With no outer layer of clothes, I was cold and couldn't quite grip the gun without shaking a little—even when holding it with two hands. When it came within ten feet of me, the bear stood up on its hind legs, giving me a full view of its eight-foot bulk. Everything else was lost to my view but the texture of its fur and its very long claws. As it moved slowly toward me, shuffling on its hind legs, I carefully aimed the gun at its chest and squeezed the trigger. The flare hit the bear between its two front legs and managed to ignite some of its fur. Startled, the animal stopped; it smelled the smoke, then turned and lumbered off toward the water. It took me three hours to stop shaking long enough to load my one remaining flare into the chamber. I had two more days to wait before the plane was scheduled to pick me up; with no serious weapon, my radio batteries dead, and fearing the bear's return, it would be a long wait. For the first time, I felt quite vulnerable.

Glen Ellen, California

I have always been drawn to the idea of the canary in the mine as a metaphor for our own human lives. The Lancashire coppy, a canary with a lovely, melodious song, became extinct between the two world wars. (Recently, it has been re-created from crossbreeds that were its offspring.) These canaries were a fairly hearty breed, able to endure contaminated air, dampness, darkness, and oxygen deprivation. It was the original test bird. Placed in cages at different levels in the mine shafts, the birds were carefully watched by miners for evidence of lethargy or impending death; silent coppies were the clearest sign of dangerous conditions in the mine.

In the course of my life's work, I used to feel much like the coppy, experiencing a dark and suffocating existence caused by ungratifying work and "needs" I thought I couldn't resist. However, instead of remaining a prisoner in this cage, I have been able to find satisfaction in my life, a sense of liberation that came when my choices were vibrant, filled with natural sound and blessed light.

For the past thirty years, I have recorded the sounds of creatures and the wild habitats in which they live. Rainforests to polar regions, high plains to desert, coral reefs to open ocean, river habitats to mangrove swamps, these are the places that make up my office. People may wonder how I can prefer the risk of snakebites, bear attacks, and gorilla fights to an existence in modern Western society. But I find it easier to embrace the uncertainty, wonder, and passions of the animal world; this is a jungle I can bear. Throughout my experiences as a musician and naturalist, I have discovered that an essential place for me is the natural wild, a place where I can leave behind the noise of my life and finally hear the sounds that speak resonantly to my soul. It is a place where my senses are truly alive and, at the same time, completely at peace.

Part I

I think I could turn

Detroit

Edgar Cayce, my mother's favorite psychic, was commissioned to do a "life reading" of me when I was six weeks old. In it, he forecast my future as "one that will be tempered with song, music, those things having to do with nature." I never saw or knew of the prediction until I was twenty-five years old, and by then, the course of my life was well underway.

I experienced the house in which I was born as a daily symphony. It was built on the corner of an intersection in north-west Detroit, an area still mostly farmland in the late 1930s. The modest-sized house had three small bedrooms, a small living room, dining room, kitchen, one-and-a-half baths, and a den which served as a library.

My room was located in the back of the house above the kitchen. It was there that the rhythm of Krause and creature life embedded itself in my memory. Open windows on both sides of the corner room let in the early morning sounds of mourning doves, frogs, wood warblers, cardinals, chickadees, vireos, robins, starlings, and crickets from the nearby fields. Inside the house at dawn, doors would creak and snap shut, plumbing would spring to life from the bathroom down the hall, and pots, plates, and silverware would rattle with the same reassuring timbre each morning from the kitchen below. Throughout the day, the women my parents hired to help clean and care for me and my sister went about their tasks, each establishing her own unique ambient performance in the process. At first, my parents hired German refugees to work for us. Then, soon after the war began, Camille, an African-American woman, was hired, and she remained with our family for many years.

There was no local preschool and few kids in the neighborhood of whom my parents approved, so I generally stayed by myself, playing in my room with small musical instruments, a marvelous train set by Lionel, Erector sets, model airplanes, or science kits. But mostly, I just listened for the muffled sounds of the daily routine coming from the washing machine or the mangle in the basement, the rush of air through the heating grates, the whirring of the old Hoover vacuum, and the gentle humming of Camille as she went about her tasks. Sometimes, during a mid-week afternoon, when my mother tucked me away for a nap, sounds of laughter and conversation from her regular canasta game would waft upstairs to the room where I lay wide awake, trying to make some sense of the sounds from the living room world below.

My parents were very strict about our behavior during mealtimes. Periodically, I was sent to my room or into the kitchen to eat with Camille for my misbehavior during dinner. Even though I felt ashamed by the punishment, I also felt relieved from having to endure the strict discipline at the table. When sent to my room, I'd lie on the floor until bedtime, vaguely aware of time only by the changing light outside and the retrograde sounds as the house was put to sleep. The whip-poor-will, bullfrog, and crickets in the adjacent field, the last flushes of the toilet and running water in the sink, the final creak of a door hinge, and the snap of a latch as the door to my parents' bedroom closed for the night were the codas for each day.

At times, before putting me to bed, my dad or mom would read me a bedtime story. But it was always the rhythmic pulse of a cricket or the voice of a distant nightjar that would lull me to sleep. In that way, I was first drawn to the sounds of the natural world, which made me feel that all was well and safe in mine. Sometimes, just before drifting off, I'd imagine having conversations with these mysterious creatures who lay just outside the grasp of my tiny hands.

My parents were terrified of animals. They were especially alarmed by the dirt and diseases creatures carried. "Why can't we have a dog (or a cat, or a hamster) like other kids?" my sister and I would ask over and over.

"They're dirty!" my mother would sniff, quickly adding, "If you want to *clean* 'em, you can have 'em."

My parents sensed unseen ferocity in animals, even in the tamest beast. My mother would pull me close to her whenever a neighborhood dog approached too closely. Both she and my dad were too stalwart to express their fear verbally, but their facial expressions and firm grip on my hand were giveaways.

The wildest creatures ever to cross our threshold were goldfish. They were easy to care for and if they died—which most did—cost only a dime to replace. We had an occasional painted turtle, which I would try to provoke into action only to have it retreat stubbornly into its shell. I soon got bored playing with them, and I'd forget to put them back in their small glass container. They'd escape under the rug or the bed, never to be seen alive again, but ultimately recovered by their decaying smell after a few weeks.

Instinctively, I loved animals. But my parents, lacking an understanding of creature life, never showed my sister or me how to properly care for those that came into our lives. And truly wild animals? Not a snake in the world was harmless. Frogs lived in muddy ponds. Birds fouled their own nests and lived in filth. Just look at robins digging in *dirt* for *worms!* These vile creatures are certainly not of our world. Early on, I adopted my parents' aversion to animals— something that took me years to overcome.

———

The first time I took a violin into my hands, it was said, I was able to play a recognizable melody. I was three-and-a-half years old at the time, and my parents were thrilled that a tune could spring from the half-sized instrument they had purchased for twenty-five dollars for their prospective wunderkind. They chose the violin because of my apparent enthusiasm after we attended a Fritz Kreisler concert. As it turned out, my level of musicianship proved to be somewhat below the expectations of both my parents and teachers. Part of the problem was my poor eyesight, which my parents were slow to notice. As a result, I gave some pretty imaginative renditions of Pleyel and simple Bach exercises.

I was, nevertheless, skilled enough to show some talent. I learned mostly by imitating my baffled teacher, who also didn't realize that I was having trouble seeing notes on the page. When composition and solfège classes were added a year later with my teacher's encouragement, my parents thought they had a prodigy on their hands— especially since my teacher was the first principal violinist in the Detroit Symphony. But once again, I was doomed to disappoint everyone. My progress was neither swift nor certain enough. For me, solace appeared somewhere on the other side of the window, outside the room where I was supposed to practice two hours a day. Relegated to my small room in the back of the house, I spent many happy hours alone with the window wide open, listening to sounds coming from myriad creatures I had yet to know.

Whenever I tried to investigate the creature world on my own or asked a question about it, my parents diverted my attention back to music—a more "civilized" preoccupation that they understood.

Early on, I learned the intricate songs and calls of some of the birds in the fields around our house; this helped me develop a discriminating ear, making the transition to music fairly easy. When more music lessons were added to what my mentors saw as a "practical" way for a three-and-a-half-year-old to spend time, the melodies of whip-poor-wills were relegated to a low priority. While I tolerated the diversion, I didn't enjoy music at this young age. My training was strictly a rigid form of "Old World" European discipline; I had no musical role model who could show me that music could be passionate or natural.

To escape, I played outside in the fields along with the other neighborhood kids, digging tunnels and searching out rabbits and frogs. Meanwhile, the house was a veritable font of discovery. Any time I was left alone, I would sneak over to the old 78 rpm record player in the living room and begin to explore. I had figured out that the needle in the player arm vibrated as a result of tracking the grooves of the records. I remember trying to run the needle along the grooves in the whorls of my thumbprints to see, if by some miracle, I could produce a musical or bird sound. As I ran my thumb back and forth across the needle, the speaker crackle and sputter was magic to hear. But just when I thought I'd made a discovery, my mother walked in and yelled at me for "ruining" the player.

This was a confusing time for me because, while I knew what I was drawn to, I had no way to express what I felt, and there was no one within the circle of my family who could guide me. But the sounds coming from the field outside my bedroom window left an impression that would continue to interest me whenever I took the time to listen. I was years away from discovering that I could actually create a life around the chirps of birds and the growls of mammals.

and live awhile with the animals...

When I was young, my dad would take me to local farms to visit the animals, or to the zoo where he would react with the same childlike delight as us kids when the lions roared or elephants swung their heads from side to side. I watched his reactions closely to see what he would do or say. As much as he'd *ooh* and *ah,* I always had the feeling that he was comfortable only when standing at some distance from the safety railing. It became clear that this was as close as he ever wished to get to "nature." In those rare moments when he'd let go of my hand and look away, I'd quickly scoot under the railing and stand nose to nose with whatever creature I could. It was then that his face would turn ashen and, in a panic, he would rush forward to pull me back behind the railing. Having both a love and fear of living things, my father passed on to me a conflict so strong it would take many years to resolve it. Still, as we watched the animals together from behind a fence, I felt he was trying to find a way to give me something he yearned to connect to, and yet, he lacked whatever courage or personal history it took to do so. The result for me was a paradoxical perception of seeing the animals, their keepers, and visitors all as prisoners of one kind or another. If he felt the same, he never expressed the irony.

On winter Sunday afternoons or during the few evenings when he wasn't too tired from working, my father would build a fire in the fireplace, seat me next to him on the floor, and read Dickens, Melville, Hawthorne, Thoreau, or Blake late into the night until I curled up and fell asleep, dreaming of the nineteenth century world he loved so well. But this wasn't the world I had to meet each new day. From that there was no escape except in fantasy.

Like the animals I have come to know through my craft, the lyricism and warmth of my dad's voice stayed with me and often helped me endure uncertain times. I vividly recall the readings of Ahab's pursuit of the great whale. Even at five or six it occurred to me that the whale was somehow us. Many years later, I would think of the great white whale when, as director of the operation that led Humphrey the humpback whale from the rivers of the San Francisco Bay back to the Pacific, my mind would return to what seemed like a safer and more secure time.

—

My father had graduated from law school and practiced law before I was born. But he left his practice to join his father in a thriving bakery supply business when a serious illness kept my grandfather from work for a considerable period of time. My dad's brother-in-law (who died several years ago) also joined the company. Shortly after the war, considerable amounts of money mysteriously disappeared from the company account. An audit made it clear that my uncle was the cause. At the time a recreational gambler, he needed funds to cover his mounting debts. So he misappropriated money from the company, forging my father's signature on checks and seriously threatening the viability of the business. When my uncle was confronted by my parents and given an ultimatum to pay it all back or go to jail, my grandfather sided with his son-in-law who, despite his actions, was allowed to remain with the company.

This surprise decision forced my dad to leave a job he badly needed. Desperate and bewildered, he stopped spending much time with my sister and me. I was ten years old then and still remember how profoundly our lives changed; overnight, it seemed. No longer did we venture to the zoo or to nearby farms to visit the animals. No longer did we take rides into the country in his beige '47 Chevy to see the fall colors or the cider pressing mills. Instead, Dad used to take me with him when he stood in the unemployment lines. A deep malaise settled around us, and my parents began to fight between themselves over issues I could not then understand.

Sometimes I'd eavesdrop while hiding near the top of the stairs, but the meaning of their heated and intense exchanges was often lost to me. Late at night, the harsh whispers would keep me awake and afraid. While I wasn't sure what was happening, and my parents didn't explain anything, I knew something was wrong. Dad became increasingly depressed and detached the more he realized he had lost his livelihood and had been betrayed by his father and his brother-in-law, two men he had respected and trusted. Trying to protect the integrity of our family, my mother stood adamant in the face of these betrayals, refusing to budge from her ever-hardened positions.

Because of my mother's unwillingness to compromise, many of our relatives and friends—particularly on my dad's side—drifted away from us. No longer did we visit our cousins on Sundays or during holidays. Even though there was rivalry between us, they had been fun to play with. I missed their companionship and their world, so different from the more serious and restrained atmosphere of our home. Not having many friends that my parents approved of, my life became even more lonely.

While this was happening, I continually dreamt of living with the creature world. At school I wrote a paper about living with the animals. I fantasized (and wrote) about how peaceful it would be to live underground and to sleep for many months during the year, just like the grizzlies I read about in books. This only made me withdraw further into a world of fantasy and daydreams. I was charmed by thoughts of living in a creature world with protective families of wolves and bears, all the while surrounded by sounds as I sang and reassured these animals through music that I wasn't there to do them harm, thus creating a mystical but wonderful bond.

Despite all the stress and family troubles, my parents hit on an idea they could develop together and struggled to build a small retail business featuring utensils for gourmet cooking and baking. In 1950, with a modest amount of money they had put away for my sister and me, they bought an old jeweler's safe for their fledgling enterprise at the estate auction of a single man who had left no heirs. We were all working at the warehouse they had rented in a depressed part of town—Dad and I were painting and rat-proofing the floor when we heard a sudden, loud scream from my mother. Rushing into the office, we found her sitting on the floor clutching a fistful of cash. With the $10,000 she had discovered in a false bottom of the safe, my parents were able to order a small inventory and purchase a used truck, while still retaining enough money for us to live on for a time.

The tension that had accumulated during my pre-teen years evaporated almost overnight as my parents recovered some measure of vitality, self-esteem, and hope. It marked the beginning of their working relationship together, building a business from scratch that would ultimately prosper. But while it brought our immediate family closer together during those difficult times, for my sister and me, the isolation from the rest of our kin seemed only to increase.

—

Our middle-class Detroit home was fairly liberal in thought and expression, if not exactly in deed. Dad often spoke in lofty terms of his love of Gandhi as a mentor of peace. As a former attorney, he admired those whom he thought best expressed notions of fairness and justice, often quoting Cardozo, Brandeis, and Darrow as examples. He spoke of unions as being the great social equalizer in our culture, necessary to bring benefits to the "little man." It was only later that I realized just how very conservative and cautious my home environment was in practice. My parents seemed fearful of exploring complex ideas, even to test and play with them. The more I tried to engage them and ask questions beyond the practical—like why we didn't have any non-Jewish or black friends—the more defensive they became, meeting my inquiries with silence or a new subject.

With constant pressure to think as they thought, I often felt somewhat humiliated and made to feel as if I were failing them. They seemed disappointed in my inadequacies, like my mediocre grades in school, my questions that flew in the face of strongly held values, or my actions to find answers for myself. Their responses were often subtle: a pursed lip; a raised eyebrow; arms folded across a chest; a tone of voice. All demonstrated that I had crossed some imaginary line between the proper and improper.

In my own way, I began to show a certain amount of contempt, strongly pressuring them to engage in discussion and debate. Frustrated and unable or unwilling to play along with the challenges, Mom would become infuriated and respond as if I had insulted her. Sometimes she'd just yell. Other times, she would strike me hard with the back of her hand—the one with the large diamond ring. Once, I was thrown down the stairs. It made her feel bad to lose control like that. Hours later, when all had been too quiet for too long, she would come to my room to see if I was all right. I always had the impression it was more to see if she was forgiven. She was.

—

By the late forties, the dirt road bordering the south side of our house had been paved, and traffic increased to the point where accidents frequently occurred day and night. My parents moved me into the bedroom nearest to the street so they could get some needed sleep in my old cater-corner room in the back. Things had changed there, too. Where fields had existed only a few years before, houses now stood; the birds were long gone, their songs replaced by muffled sounds of radios and new televisions the neighbors had purchased—their windows and a brick wall not ten feet from where I used to gaze across fields that stretched, it seemed, for miles.

I didn't mind the room change so much at first. The new room was a little bigger. However, the sounds of creature life were replaced by constant traffic noises. During these turbulent times in my childhood, I remember how the music of Bessie Smith, the Modern Jazz Quartet, Leadbelly, Burl Ives, and Marais and Miranda opened up a world that temporarily carried me beyond the limits of our tiny piece of Detroit property. Because this was not my parents' favorite music, I could only listen to these records when my parents were out of the house.

It was in the world of such disparate sounds that I found some sense of well-being and confidence, although it was clear to me then that some component was missing. It would take some time before I finally began to piece the puzzle together.

they are so placid and self-contained,

While the music we heard as a family was often restricted to the classics, the influence of radio and the records passed along by family friends somehow made my adolescent life bearable. By the early fifties, before my early teens, most of my musical interests focused on jazz, pop, blues, and occasional folk music being performed locally. "Amazing Grace" was one of the first tunes I learned outside of the prescribed music in our family. Sung by Camille, the tune often inspired me to skip Sunday Hebrew classes and sneak into her church just to hear the choir perform. The sheer energy of gospel music brought joy and excitement to my life as a very timid and self-absorbed child. I was enchanted by those moments.

My musical roots and interests were fairly eclectic. By the mid-forties, some friends of my parents, whose house we would frequently visit, introduced me to jazz, theater, and pop music with a passion I had never experienced at home. Three things drew me to jazz as a kid: it was much less stiff and controlled than the music my parents endorsed; it seemed to be much more visceral and therefore natural; and, finally, it was something I understood intuitively that my parents didn't, which was liberating because it gave me special territory that I could call my own.

By the time I was thirteen, the violin had become an ordeal. So I quit and tried a number of other instruments: cello, bass, viola, harp—pretty much all the strings—until one summer at a camp in Ontario, I heard someone play the guitar and thought I had gone to heaven! I studied hard and quickly learned every style of the time—rock, jazz, classical—and actually became a fair reader and performer. The music of Bertha Chippie Hill, Louis Armstrong, Earl Fatha' Hines, Fats Waller, Billie Holiday, Bix Beiderbecke, and Bessie Smith were all familiar to me before I entered ninth grade. By the time I was fifteen, I was playing guitar and amplified ukulele in a dance band and having a great deal of fun.

The guitar, of course, made my parents crazy. For one thing, they viewed it as a blue-collar instrument—a class they definitely were striving to exceed—and certainly not something to have fun with. Second, it was taking all my time; I wanted nothing to do with the family. When they went out to dinner, I wanted to stay home, listen to rock and roll or Andrés Segovia, and practice. Nothing they could offer was more enticing than playing guitar. It was the first thing I could do completely on my own.

———

My high school was located in the northwest section of Motown. I spent most of my time outside of school bopping down the street in a chopped and blocked '51 powder blue Ford convertible—certainly not mine—with the old tube radio blaring Bill Haley and the Comets or Bo Diddley. The local deejays of the time (like Robin Seymore, for whom the song, "When The Red, Red, Robin Comes Bob, Bob, Bobbin' Along" was written) called out tunes that made the playlists. When jazz performers came to town, a bunch of us would gather outside the local clubs, like the Minor Key on Livernois, pressing our ears to the back doors because we were too young to get in. Sooner or later, the bouncer would send us on our way; but sometimes, when his mood was right or when the crowd was light, he'd crack open the door just enough to let us hear performances of some of the all-time greats, such as the Modern Jazz Quartet, Eric Dolphy, or Miles Davis.

Usually, I was able to get my musical fixes only from records—those recordings that were passed along by friends who were finished listening or bored with the stuff, or when I had a birthday. My parents didn't have enough money to spend on "frivolous" purchases like "unusual" music. "Not practical!" my mother would sniff, adding nothing more substantial.

My parents had only a limited interest in music other than the albums they bought or programs selected on the radio. Some of their friends and a few of my high school buddies had a much wider musical range. I guess my mom's response was more academic—endorsing only the music we "should" listen to and know. Bach or Beethoven were at the top of the list; Chopin and Rachmaninov were her romantic favorites because of their beautiful melody lines. She never expressed any particular desires for other styles. Neither parent ever suggested we go hear jazz, rock and roll, or any of the pop artists who frequently came to town to perform. My parents disliked Elvis Presley when he burst on the scene. Even Harry Belafonte was looked upon by my mom with a combination of desire and suspicion: "Why does he have to wear his shirt open like that?" she hissed at my dad, who sat on the couch, puffing on his cigar and staring straight ahead. My dad, on the other hand, although his tastes were fairly limited, seemed to respond to the spirit of music and occasionally would even express some emotion over a great performance. It was the enthusiasm of their few music-loving friends that added the necessary juice to my teenage life.

Sometime in the early sixties, my parents' jazz-collecting friends, then retired and divesting themselves of extra belongings, packed the remainder of their collection of rare 78s and shipped it to me. One day, a large semi-trailer pulled up outside my small Brooklyn Heights apartment and dumped a pallet of large, heavy cartons on the sidewalk. To this day, I still haven't listened to all of this material, although much of it has been cleaned up and transferred to compact disc. It is a remarkable accumulation: music from Louisiana bayous dating back to the twenties, blues, early Armstrong, Klezmer music, Burl Ives, Marais & Miranda, Leadbelly, and even some jazz performances Doris Day did when she was a teenager that were far more exciting than her later work.

Because some of the collection had been given to me over the years beginning in the mid-forties, as a teenager in the mid-1950s, I already had a strong hunch that there was much to be discovered in what was then called "ethnic" music. It was also a time when folk music was becoming the rage, first popularized by Burl Ives, Woody Guthrie, Pete Seeger, the Weavers, Josh White, Belafonte, and the Kingston Trio. Some of it was deemed politically "safe." Some of it was seen as more dangerous—like songs containing ideas that there might be better ways to connect with people and our environment than by killing, maiming, or polluting—stirring indignation from some quarters and discomfort in my parents.

New York

My family would frequently travel to Manhattan by overnight train. For me it was the heart of magic—a fierce contrast to the flat, uninspired environment of Detroit. It was on one such trip, when I was seventeen, that I first saw the Weavers during their 1955 Town Hall concert, the first of many comeback events. The offer to take me to a Weavers concert was quite unusual for my parents—a departure from the normal and safe classical performances they usually dragged me to. I felt their apprehension but was also deeply touched by their outreach.

The air in the hall was thick with excitement and expectation. When the Weavers began to sing, the atmosphere was palpable. I couldn't believe that their live appearances could exceed the quality of the recordings I had all but worn out at home. In spite of Joseph McCarthy's attempts to silence members of the group, they had managed to persevere and survive with their freshness and political passion intact. The crowd was on its feet most of the time. Even standing on my seat, I rarely caught a glimpse of the group that night. But I sure as hell could hear the music, and I can still recall the feeling of love and energy in the air that night. And for a fleeting moment, I even imagined myself on the stage, guitar in hand, singing with them.

Ann Arbor

While a student at the University of Michigan in the mid-fifties, I joined the Folklore Society, which immediately caused me to be blackballed from the fraternities I had mistakenly thought I might like to join. Those of us in the Folklore Society aggressively sang folk songs and hustled dates with our guitars. I played the instrument as hard and as loud as I could—and not necessarily very well, either. But apparently just well enough to improve my social life. We had weekly meetings—"hoots"—and occasionally split off into smaller performing groups to play at fraternity parties and other campus functions. Our youthful energies were largely spent strutting for attention: who was the best guitar performer, who could sing the most French or Spanish songs, or who was the most radical, the most angry, the most victimized, the most underprivileged, and, of course, the most "hip." The men soon discovered that these displays had a tendency to attract women—the not-too-subtle subtext of most of what was going on.

Among the members of the Society was Al Young, then a published poet, short-story writer, and essayist, not to mention a talented vocalist, guitar player, and performer; Bill McAdoo, then a devoted Marxist; and Joe Dassin, son of Jules (director of the film,

Never on Sunday), a singer and raconteur. With each of us expressing various degrees of political passion, we felt that our music would help change a world we saw as corrupt; several of us laid our asses on the line, traveling south to engage in voter registration, or to Washington to address anti-nuclear issues, disarmament, and Cuba. In later years, Al Young became a Stegner Fellow, taught at Stanford, and published several novels and books of poetry. McAdoo became a colleague of Malcolm X's, only to end up later on Wall Street as a broker. And Dassin, after enjoying a successful career in France, committed suicide one night in his Paris apartment.

A few in the Society began to assume the mantle of being the most hip and politically relevant. This meant, of course, enviously turning against the very things in the folk genre that were gentle and well-motivated: specifically against spokespeople with some kind of moral center who were finally getting attention for their art. Peer pressure demanded that we view these important folk musicians as not imaginative enough, not "folk" enough, not "ethnic" enough, or not whatever-came-to-mind enough. We also needed to create objects of scorn. In this way, the Weavers and Seeger became targets for the most radical elements of the Folklore Society. No one in his or her right mind would mention the Kingston Trio or the Limelighters in a positive light. Many in the group would never be seen at their concerts. The music itself had little to do with the issue; the musicians were targeted simply for making money.

Some fellows in the Folklore Society spent a good deal of time defending their political turf with fist fights. Mostly, the battles were about which songs were most politically relevant or how they should be performed. We sang of peace and harmony and holding hands around the world, but would still end up beating on each other about the most inane things. "If I Had a Hammer" was written by capitalists, and by singing it, you were so labeled. "Midnight Special," on the other hand, because it sprang from the oppressed, showed your affinity to more substantive issues. "I'll squash you!" McAdoo screamed one day as an unwitting white fellow dared to play a C major 7th chord on his guitar, thus desecrating the sanctity of "Midnight Special." Stepping outside the room, they duked it out and both disappeared for the rest of the evening.

Then there were political discussions. Middle-class whites in the Folklore Society were made to feel inadequate for not having suffered quite enough. But some of us saw through all this bullshit pretty early in the game and moved on to more interesting matters—like the wonderful varieties of music that were beginning to emerge from everywhere around us.

A few of us from the core members of the Society formed a performance group. It consisted of Al Young, Bill McAdoo, Joe Dassin (who sometimes appeared and sometimes didn't, depending on the current state of his female companionship), and me. Despite all the heartache brought about by ego trips and ignorance, the music prevailed, and we generally rose above our differences when onstage. The music had the effect of calming and reassuring us, and we always felt better for having performed it together. To keep active, we were constantly forced to look for new material. It was a time when wonderful music from the American South and Africa was beginning to have a voice—even appealing to uptight academics in the music department.

I recall no particular feeling of lightness then, just intensity. The songs of the birds had become only a distant echo. I was distracted by what I was told I should be doing with my life by my parents, professors, friends, lovers, and the media. My slow coming of age was painful: music was the bandaid.

I stand and look at them long and long.

Whenever I wasn't studying, which was the maximum amount of time I could get away with, I drove into Detroit to hang out at recording sessions wherever the great guitarist Joe Messina was playing. Sometimes he could be found at Motown recording sessions in the garage of Berry Gordy, Motown's founder. Other times, Messina worked at a downtown television studio, WXYZ, from which the "Soupy Sales Show" was broadcast. After I studied with him for a time and became good enough, I would occasionally be asked to sit in and play music with the studio groups, even earning enough extra money to cover expenses at school. Between sessions I kept looking for aural ideas I could claim as my own and incorporate into my work.

For this influence, I turned to Moe Asch at Folkways, one of my early mentors, who had released many new collections of music from around the world—Africa, Eastern Europe, Asia—and material from the Alan Lomax collection of the American South. From these recordings I could find ways to learn new material and incorporate fresh rhythms, harmonies, and instrumental textures into my music. This music gave me some insight into what my rather insular life lacked; I began to get a window on the greater world and I was an eager student.

New York

In the late fifties, while I was still in college, I formed a duo with Carole Werner, daughter of the vice president of NBC-TV, Mort Werner. (He was also Dave Garroway's manager on the side, in the days before conflict of interest was an issue.) A network insider who knew all about the workings of the "Quiz Show," Mort had significant influence (we needed all we could get) and landed us a spot on the "Today Show," performing over several months. Because the phobia from the McCarthy era was still strong, the show staff, over our objections, always picked the most innocuous material for us to perform.

Before one show, I was handed a piece of paper—a loyalty oath that we were required to sign before we went on the air. It stated that we were not Communists, never knew a Communist, and wouldn't know one if we saw one. I asked the producer if everyone on the set had signed it, and he told me, "Not everyone." Ten seconds before air-time, tiny scraps of the document drifted from my hands to the floor like snow. There was nothing NBC could do. With a face full of rage and contempt, the floor producer signaled our attention to the camera, and we launched into what was to be my last appearance on television for nearly fifteen years.

The Weavers and Pete Seeger were the first popular American artists to borrow from the traditions collected by Moe Asch and Alan Lomax, one of the most influential ethnomusicologists and collectors of the twentieth century. The Weavers had a string of hits in the early fifties: "Tzena, Tzena," "So Long It's Been Good to Know Ya," "On Top of Old Smoky," "Good Night Irene," and "Wimoweh." Their performances were exciting, and they made the music sound easy to sing and play. They incorporated freshness and electricity into their shows still unmatched today in any medium; their sense of theater became extremely influential on me. The Weavers' music was the first I had heard with strong messages, and I particularly liked the intimacy of their performances.

Folk music began to work for me on a number of different levels that other idioms couldn't quite match. It was compelling, it was inspiring, and it touched listeners in very personal ways. However, with graduation only a year away, I needed to find a job, whether the Folklore Society approved or not. Every artist booked within 100 miles of Ann Arbor had to contend with me backstage after their performance, where I begged for a chance to play backup guitar. The only one who agreed—well, sort-of—was Bob Gibson.

Chicago

In May 1959, Bob Gibson came to Detroit to give a concert. While I was in college, I had learned every Bob Gibson technique simply because I was drawn to the pure energy of his performances. I idolized Gibson and thought he was remarkable. He played guitar and banjo closer to Seeger's style than almost anyone else I had heard.

After the concert, I went backstage with my guitar and sat outside his dressing room, playing every lick Gibson had performed that night. Eventually, Gibson came over to where I was playing and said, "You seem to know all my songs."

"Yeah," I said confidently, "and I hear you're looking for a backup guitarist. You got one."

"Well, I can't give you much money, but I'm booked at the Gate of Horn in June, and I need some help." he said. "Why don't you come and we'll see how things go? Oh, by the way, I can pay five bucks a night. But you gotta get your ass to Chicago on your own."

Sounded like good luck! With all the clothes my guitar case would hold, I jumped a freight heading west out of Detroit; I was making good time until I was detrained by a guard in South Bend. So I wandered around for a while until I hitched a ride with a truck driver to the Loop. I arrived in Chicago's Old Town without enough money in my pocket to eat.

Al Grossman, Gibson's manager, had an office a few blocks from the Gate. Bob had suggested we meet there. His office, located in an old brick building, had posters of Gibson, Odetta, and other famous people Grossman managed (prior to his management of Bob Dylan and Peter, Paul, and Mary). When Grossman's secretary finally sauntered into the chairless waiting room, I asked if Al was there. "Yeah, he's in a room down the hall," she mumbled, motioning to an unlit hallway.

"Well, I'm here to meet Bob Gibson," I said.

"I wouldn't know," she answered. "He never told me anything about your arrival or any meeting."

"Well, Gibson told me to show up. I'm supposed to play with him tonight. Open at the Gate of Horn."

She shrugged indifferently and told me to walk down the hall and speak with Al. Following her instructions, I walked into a room where, to my youthful amazement, Al was in a bed with a woman! He brought his hand up from under the sheet for me to shake. Wet and sticky, his handshake was memorable. "Wait for me in the office and I'll talk with you when I'm done," I heard him mutter.

I left—feeling a bit sick—and sat on the floor in the waiting room. The secretary, seeing that I was bored and anxious, offered to let me use the phone. I called my mother to tell her I had arrived safely, then left a message at my grandfather's office, inviting him to come to the club.

Gibson finally arrived around four in the afternoon. At first, he looked surprised because he had either forgotten his invitation or didn't really expect me to show up. (I suspected he'd had a little too much smoke when we had met in Detroit.) Then he motioned to me and said, "Come on, we're going to walk over to the club for a sound check. Bring everything you got."

Walking down the street, Gibson grabbed my shoulder and motioned to an old man just ahead of us. "You see this guy with the white hair? Let's follow him. I think he's gonna go into that record store."

We followed the white-haired man as he turned into the store. Approaching him, Gibson said, "Bernie, come here. I want to introduce you to somebody. Bernie, this is Carl Sandburg."

Catching my breath, I struggled to say something intelligent but was silent from shock. To my surprise, Sandburg grinned and invited us to his place, which happened to be just down the street. We hung out with Sandburg for an hour or so, drinking iced tea, singing a little, and talking a lot.

Late in the afternoon, Bob and I left Sandburg's apartment after he assured us he would come to the opening. Then we went to the Gate of Horn to do the sound check. A fragile-looking young woman with long, black hair, bare feet, and marvelous, enigmatic eyes sat alone in the corner of the empty room. I fell in love with her in a nanosecond. It was her first gig out of Cambridge, and she was the opening act for Gibson. I sat down next to her at the table, and we began playing guitar together, exchanging tunes, and singing to one another. Except for a hello in passing at an airport, Joan Baez and I have never since exchanged a word.

After the sound check, I phoned my grandfather again. He told me he'd already heard from my mother and she was unhappy with my choice of occupations. I was really proud of my first job but could hear in his voice that he didn't share my enthusiasm. I tried to forget about our conversation as I prepared for my professional debut.

That evening, every seat in the Gate was filled; people were lined up against the back wall and sat on the stairs, spilling out into the street. Baez finished her set to mild applause, and then it was our turn. Walking up on the stage with Gibson and playing the opening tune was one of the most emotionally charged moments of my life. In my mind, I was finally a pro, and with every successive measure of music, I felt more assured, empowered, and vindicated.

Toward the end of the first song, I caught a glimpse of three figures elbowing people aside as they forced their way toward the stage. I couldn't see very clearly because of the spotlight glare and the haze. But I did notice that two of them didn't stop shoving until they reached the lip of the stage. As we launched into the opening bars of the second tune, these two goons jumped up on the stage and shoved their way past the mics and cables to where I was standing. One grabbed my guitar and the other gripped my arm; they lifted me off the platform, through the room, up the stairs, and out the door—my feet barely touching the ground during the whole transaction. I thought they were cops and felt utterly helpless. I had no idea what I had done.

Dragging me outside, one of these jerks pushed me up against the wall and pinned my arms. The other stood in the background, gripping my guitar by the sound hole. It was only then that I saw my grandfather standing in the shadows. He gave a nod. The fellow holding my guitar smashed it to pieces on a fire hydrant. Then my grandfather bounded over to me in a rage, and with one goon still restraining me, he slapped me hard across the head and screamed, "No grandson of mine is going to play these dives with whores and prostitutes!"

After the beating, the two thugs, hired through some of my grandfather's "better" acquaintances from his Chicago Prohibition days, hustled me into a limo and drove me out to Midway Airport where a waiting plane flew me back to Detroit. I was so embarrassed and furious that I never spoke with my grandfather again. Since my mother was a knowledgeable co-conspirator, I couldn't bring myself to speak with her until several months later. While we endured a civil relationship, from that point on, any residual trust I may have felt before that incident was shattered forever. As for Gibson, about twenty-five years later we met for breakfast in Los Angeles. I asked if he remembered that night in Chicago. After I told him the story, he just shrugged and remarked, "So, that's what happened?"

They do not sweat

After I graduated from college in 1960, I went to work for NBC in New York. As an associate producer on "Monitor Radio," a weekend AM radio series, I was responsible for scheduling music for our segment of the program as well as auditioning newly-released single tunes hustled by heavily-perfumed music promoters in sharkskin suits. The promoters offered the network producers many incentives. These perks were not always limited to cash under the table or expensive meals; exotic sex and serious drugs were also staple offerings on the menu. Even though I occasionally programmed some of their music when it fit, I never went for the perks, probably because I didn't like the options. I do have to admit that I was tempted, though, as I was being paid only eighty-five dollars a week.

I soon learned that there was an unwritten record playlist mandate from the head production office. It went something like this: only one black singer, male or female, could be programmed in any one hour; no more than three female performances in any one hour; instrumentals were ok only if performed by recognized white orchestras; folk music was a Communist plot. When I asked why the mandate existed—apparently something you could do only once in your 1960s corporate career—I was told stations in the South would object and cancel the programming. However, I continued to program Ella Fitzgerald, Nancy Wilson, Barbra Streisand (who was actually considered too upbeat by the senior producers), Ray Charles, and Belafonte more frequently than allowed.

After a couple of months, Max Loeb, the program director, had enough of my efforts to change network broadcasting, and I was hauled into his office. In spite of Loeb's directive to stop playing "nigger music," I refused to stop programming the artists I liked and was soon fired.

After NBC, I began performing in some of the clubs in Greenwich Village. During the summer of 1960, I met up with a folk duo called Art (Podell) and Paul (Potash). Their manager, a moonlighting program director from a Manhattan radio station, offered to match my NBC salary if I would back up the group on bass, guitar, banjo, and mandolin. As part of the bargain, I was also required to be their road manager.

Dayton

After our engagement in New York at the Roundtable as the opening act for Mabel Mercer, we played one small club in Dayton, Ohio, the Racquet Club. We were making so little money that we had to share one tiny room in a cheap motel. Somehow we managed to get three beds into a room that was large enough for only one double. The lack of space, fresh air, and discipline had us at each other's throats, and after a few days we had a huge three-way fight. Nothing serious, really. But Podell broke his toe when it got caught in the bedsprings of one of the hideaways, ending the fight. That same night, Buddy Hackett, for whom we were the opening act, grabbed a drunk patron by the shirt collar, dragged him into the parking lot, and beat the shit out of him for making some anti-Semitic remarks. This ended the gig for all of us and closed down the club.

I went back to Detroit for a short time because a close childhood friend of mine had cancer, and I wanted to be with him. Danny died after a few months—the first in a string of close male friends lost over the course of my life. I didn't wait around for the funeral because I couldn't face any more grief. Instead, I loaded my VW with all my earthly belongings and drove south to the Ohio Turnpike. At the on-ramp, I flipped a coin. Heads, east. Tails, west. Except for gas, I never stopped until I arrived in Boston.

Cambridge

There was a girl in college in Boston who I had dated in my mid-teens, and I had the misfortune to think I was madly in love with her. Her father, an arrogant fellow with much higher sights for his daughter than this dreamer, did everything he could to keep us apart, including playing on my family's misfortunes in the late forties. On a postcard, she wrote that she wanted to marry someone "who earned $10,000 a year and had a place in the community." I was mortified for failing to win her over and grew extremely depressed in this new city. I needed to do something that made me feel good.

Again, I returned to what I knew: music. The folk music scene in Boston and Cambridge was chaotic. Music heard on television or radio came mostly from artists willing to sign a loyalty oath; obviously, the best music wasn't broadcast. Although there was wonderful material coming from clubs, these artists had no way to reach the larger public. Recordings were just beginning to play a major role in folk music.

Television shows like "Hootenanny," a variety show featuring folk music, began to gain mainstream popularity while I was living in Cambridge. The homogenized, abstracted music on the show was what the larger public knew as folk music. A number of groups were "clean." Outfitted in striped shirts, khaki pants with little buckles on the back, blond hair in brush-cuts, and boat-neck sweaters, most of them knew just three or four chords and could sing in only a couple of keys. The Highwaymen and the Kingston Trio come first to mind. With the exception of Dylan, Pete Seeger, the Weavers, and Joan Baez, many of these folk groups lacked originality. Since the Weavers weren't allowed public media access, the Kingston Trio was copying their material without acknowledgment; the Highwaymen, in turn, were copying the Kingstons; and the New Christy Minstrels, Gateway Singers, and the Brothers Four were copying everyone else.

Despite what was happening on television and the radio, I was still committed to working within the music industry. In late 1961, I managed to get a job as an FM disc jockey at a small station in Framingham, Massachusetts; I worked six hours a night, six nights a week, for sixty-five dollars a week. During the day, I was able to meet some people from the larger city stations, and within a few months I was working in Boston at WBZ in the promotion department. I started taking classes at MIT as part of Westinghouse's executive training program. I liked the deal because I didn't have to go to the office every day, and I wasn't committed to work full-time until after graduation. At the time, I was working as a head of radio market research, taking classes, working for Manny Greenhill with his concert promotions at Folklore Productions, singing at night at local clubs, and teaching guitar in my spare time. The pay at the station was so meager that I had no choice but to hold down several jobs, leaving almost no time to sleep between work, school, and dates.

and whine about their condition,

I was quite impatient with myself during this period, probably because I was seeking recognition rather than happiness and fulfillment. Finally, it was the avuncular Manny at Folklore Productions who took an interest in my life and gave me some guidance through his example. He actively encouraged me to look at life with a measure of hope. Manny had a wry sense of humor that he brought to the office, making work fun and rewarding to me for the first time. This was quite a change from WBZ, where the program manager had just put a .45 to his head and decorated the walls of his apartment with fragments of cerebral tissue and skull bone.

I worked with Manny for a year and a half, managing the office, typing, booking some talent, selling ad space in local ethnic newspapers, and answering the phone. I spent most of 1961 setting up an annual folk concert series around the Boston area, including performers such as Peggy and Pete Seeger, Joan Baez, New Lost City Ramblers, Doc Watson, Odetta, Jeannie Redpath, Ramblin' Jack Elliott, Jesse Fuller, Flatt and Scruggs, and the Alfred Deller Consort. I loved the grassroots, traditional feeling of these groups and felt that there was an honesty and substance to their performances that many of the more polished groups lacked. By the time we sponsored the Weavers on the program, I thought that I had developed some pretty definite tastes in music and performance styles.

While I attended most of the other concerts, I avoided the Weavers. I had seen many of their shows and felt that they weren't radical enough for me—although to be fair, I hadn't the vaguest idea what the radical standard *du jour* was supposed to be. Since the Weavers weren't producing much new material, I naively believed that they were becoming tired and a bit boring. I thought Erik Darling and Frank Hamilton, Pete Seeger's successors, brought some musical sparkle to the instrumental and vocal areas of the group. Erik, however, seemed to be the only one of the Seeger replacements whose performances and additional material were inspired. When I'd try to discuss the Weavers with Manny, he thought I was generally full of shit about those issues, and he was probably right. He had the good sense and grace to laugh it off and not to take things too seriously.

On the night of the Weavers' October 1962 concert at MIT, I went to Club 47 and performed a satirical set based on the Weavers' songs. I was up onstage in the middle of a half-contemptuous rewrite of "If I Had a Hammer" when I saw Lee Hays of the Weavers laughing in the audience. Realizing that my attempt at satire was hideously stupid, I became flustered and thankfully missed a few choice lyrics. Lee thought it was all very amusing. Catching me completely off guard, Lee later approached me and said that the Weavers were auditioning for the Seeger chair and a Carnegie Hall reunion concert coming up in May. He asked me to submit an audition tape.

A few weeks later, after learning every tune from their records, I cranked out a tape with seven or eight numbers. I figured, what the hell. I was broke, nothing was happening, and I certainly had nothing to lose. When I learned that musicians such as Eric Weissberg ("Dueling Banjos") were vying for the spot, I was rightly concerned that my guitar and banjo techniques were not sharp or fluent enough. Although I was a quick study and could fake styles pretty well, I didn't think I had a chance. However, strongly influenced by Lee, the other members of the group asked me to come to New York for a live audition as a finalist.

I was never told exactly how the final decision was made, but I somehow got the job. At first, Lee Hays became my mentor and guide. He was a literary man of sharp intellect and wit, and he had written many of the great songs of the period such as "Wasn't That a Time," "Darlin' Corey," "Kisses Sweeter Than Wine"—some of them with Pete Seeger. Lee was terrifically generous, supportive, and helpful in many ways. But the other side of his character was also apparent. His puffy face, lusterless skin, and slightly yellowed eyes suggested a serious drinking problem. He also seemed uncertain about his sexuality, making for many stressful moments—particularly where his expectations of our relationship were concerned.

New York

When I arrived from Cambridge in January 1963, I was too broke to get my own apartment. Lee and Harold Leventhal, the group's manager, suggested I move in with Lee for a while. I was expected not only to fill the shoes of Pete and Erik, but I was also supposed to look after Lee—something I hadn't bargained for. As time passed, Harold made his expectations clear, and I became increasingly unhappy and distracted.

I was never at ease in Lee's Brooklyn Heights digs on Willow Street. For one thing, the apartment was small and very dark. For another, Lee, a heavy smoker, always kept the windows tightly closed. Norman Mailer, his upstairs neighbor, would often hammer away on his bongos late into the night. There was no lock on my bedroom door, and Lee would slip in unannounced, sometimes when I was entertaining a female date—always apologizing, always gawking just a little too long, always with a strong smell of liquor on his breath. He would send me weird, ribald pictures and letters, then take them back when I was gone. He would also rifle through my few belongings, sometimes stealing personal letters and other items when I was away.

Feeling trapped, I struggled to hold things together. I didn't have much money and couldn't afford the independence I needed to prepare for the performances. Much to Lee's disappointment, I managed to get a small apartment just around the corner. But it didn't help much. In the middle of the night, I'd see Lee scurrying down the block after dropping more weird pictures and notes into my mailbox. I felt isolated and had nowhere to turn for help. When I brought these problems to Harold's attention, my concerns were dismissed. Harold wanted to give Lee a reason to continue living and working, which meant proceeding, however we could, with the Weavers. Feeling completely undermined and betrayed, I knew I had to get out of the city and as far from Hays's apartment as possible.

Beacon, NY

In the spring of 1963, I went to stay with Pete Seeger at his home in Beacon, north of New York City on the Hudson River. I was very touched by the way he and Toshi, his wife, forged their lives together. Pete expressed his strong sense of moral certitude in everything he did or said; this was inspiring to a person like me who was still trying to find a personal source of expression. For the moment, it helped me to enjoy the task at hand, and it centered me musically. Pete was able to provide some invaluable pointers about how to give music a message and use the media to get it across; his message was one of love that went well beyond the banal.

I wanted to learn some of Pete's banjo and performance techniques and thought I could actually capture some of his magic by hanging out and learning some of his style. I also hoped I could learn a sense of Pete's amazing musical grace. Was I ever wrong! Even with youthful naiveté, for me to expect that I could learn to be Pete Seeger, learn what he knew and how he did it, or capture a fraction of his sensibilities and instrumental touch demonstrated a profound lack of judgment bordering on the insane.

I slept in the barn next to the house. Except for summer camp, it was the first time I had lived outside the city in a rural environment. All night long the mice scampered through the walls and across the ceiling. With the racket made by the mice, I couldn't sleep, so I would entertain myself by looking through the Seeger family photo albums I found in cardboard boxes.

On those cold mornings, Pete would come get me before sunrise, and we'd go chop wood and sing Leadbelly, lining out songs like we were the Hudson River Valley chain gang. During the evenings, we'd sit by the fireplace, singing and playing for a few hours. Pete would throw back his head like he was performing at Carnegie, rarely making personal or eye contact. Bewildered by his aloofness, I kept my mouth shut, endured my misgivings, and learned what I could. (Looking back on this period, I would give anything for another crack at that moment—one of the few in my life I'd want to relive.) After a few weeks of working together, we drove into the city for rehearsals with the rest of the group. Pete would lead our caravan, dropping my fare into the toll booth receptacle as we moved toward the city. No one had ever done that for me before. Within minutes of crossing the bridge, I was already missing the fresh air of Beacon.

New York

During March and April of 1963, Ronnie, Freddie, Frank, Erik, Lee, Pete, and I would meet at the old Vanguard Records studio on Fourteenth Street several days a week. Pete introduced "Guantanamera" to the group along with a few Dylan songs. The Dylan material and songs by other writers were rejected because the group couldn't seem to grasp it musically. After seeing Pete's suggestions shot down, I kept my Dylan, Dave Van Ronk, and Bonnie Dobson song suggestions to myself. I immediately recognized that none of the songs I had brought with me fit into the tight, southern Baptist church harmonies that formed the Weavers' unique sound signature.

"Guantanamera" worked, though. I wonder if it would have survived if Americans had known that their favorite hit was written by one of Fidel Castro's favorite poets, José Martí; that the original version of the song was similar to the American sophomoric couplet, "There once was a man from Nantucket..."; and that the title meant "Whore of Guantanamo," a snide rejoinder to Americans serving at the base and dedicated to the Cuban women forced to service Americans stationed at the eastern tip of the island. It wasn't too long after the Weavers' arrangement was recorded that it was copped note for note and word for word by a studio group from Los Angeles who got ultimate credit for the hit. The Weavers, still stigmatized by blacklist issues, couldn't get their version on the air. (It didn't help matters much that the marketing folks at Vanguard weren't terribly effective with the media of the day.)

From the deal I made for myself with the Weavers, I obviously knew nothing about the business, either. I signed a contract to perform with the group for $150 per week, which seemed to be an enormous amount of money at the time. I was given no royalty participation on recordings, nor any perks other than health insurance, but I was still convinced that the deal was generous and that I had a secure future as a performer. It didn't take me long to figure out that I'd been had. A healthcare provider for Lee would have earned my weekly salary in one day, and I was serving in both capacities.

To continue holding the Weavers and Lee together, Harold arranged the Carnegie Hall reunion, accurately calculating the media attention it would get and how electrifying the experience would be for the audience. During the concert, I sang "Motherless Child" with Ronnie as a duet and performed a guitar solo, the theme from "Black

Orpheus." Ronnie, Hellerman, Lee, Pete, and I sang "Guantanamera." But my performance wasn't notable. I was too nervous and had little performing experience—something I tried to convey to Lee many times before I joined the group. But he wouldn't listen to my concerns and, instead, kept reassuring me that, with his guidance, it would all work out.

The reviews, as they say, were tepid. It was my first time onstage and the intimidation, pressures, and distractions were overwhelming. My parents, who were against my performing, especially with a perceived radical group like the Weavers, attended nonetheless, with mixed feelings of pride and trepidation: at least their son was performing at Carnegie Hall. My grandfather, who had facilitated the Chicago episode, could be heard on the Vanguard Records concert master tapes snoring somewhere in the orchestra section at the front of the hall.

After the performance, the group took a long summer break and then booked a few concerts, one or two a week, mostly on weekends, the only time Lee would agree to perform. We almost never rehearsed. Lee was often too hungover and sick to leave his apartment, canceling at the last moment. Fred and Ronnie were dealing with personal issues and frustrations. It seemed that the members were not able to tolerate much of one another's presence. There was always an undercurrent of tension when we finally did get together. Tempers were short, and when there weren't disagreements, a disparaging attitude was evident everywhere—often directed at me for reasons I would never quite understand but began to take personally. When their expectations of me finally surfaced, the original members came at me with a level of hostility that I was unprepared to deal with at twenty-five years of age.

I was mostly left to rehearse alone, playing to previously recorded albums, getting together with the group only moments before we went on stage. This made me feel quite unsure of myself. Disconnected and lonely, I had almost nowhere to turn for reassurance.

I sensed that Fred, Ronnie, and Lee were getting to the point where they got no pleasure from each other or their work. Even though our performances were well received, it soon became clear to me and everyone else that I was not to become the glue that would hold them together. I once overheard Fred remark during a radio interview that I offered nothing particularly germane to the group. Although I was offended and humiliated by this public assertion, I never questioned him about his remark and kept my anger to myself. Ronnie was having lots of physical problems during that period, causing her a great deal of pain and discomfort. However, she was usually kind and would often offer suggestions and support.

Despite the offstage distractions, onstage no group was more professional than the Weavers. They exuded a vitality and put across songs in ways I have never experienced before or since with any other group. The performances were charged with excitement without the fancy production tricks that most groups need today. They were dramatic, vigorous, and magical. One thing that never flagged was the incredible love the group was able to convey to audiences no matter where we performed or under what physical or emotional condition the group members were in. The Weavers came from a performance tradition of responsibility that reached well beyond simple presentations of the music. The "show" was immensely important to them. This theatrical sense of integrity and respect for the audience was a lesson I would carry with me into the future.

Chicago

The final concert in January 1964 marked the end of one of America's truly great performance teams, and there was a great deal of sadness backstage. We had scheduled the concert for an earlier date, but it had been canceled by weather and national grief over the Kennedy assassination. There was a whole lot of commotion from the press swarming all around; Studs Terkel was there and interviewed us. I vividly recall the stress I felt when the back of my pants ripped only five minutes before curtain, and I had to scramble to close the seam with gaffing tape.

Although I was relieved to be finished, I didn't want the concert to end because I had no clear idea what I would do after the breakup. I had come to the Weavers from a diverse musical background. I had studied music, knew many styles, and was comfortable playing several stringed instruments. I loved sound but was never really happy as a performing musician. However, it was what I knew. Alternative careers in the family business, law, or medicine were, to me, not viable options, and I was overcome with anxiety just trying to imagine myself in those roles.

They do not lie awake in the dark

New York

During my brief tenure with the Weavers, I was uncertain about my own commercial aspirations. On the one hand, I was disappointed with the group and myself because I wanted them to be very successful. In fact, I wanted to play a role in that success so they could find new reasons to perform. I hoped to be seen as a valued contributor, and, not least of all, so I could qualify for a more generous participation. I wanted to bring material to them that would make them prosperous again. On the other hand, I just wanted things to go on the way they were. I had simply desired modest gains and the comfort of more than one or two concert performances a week. I didn't realize until much later how fundamentally lazy and frightened I had been.

I knew that the Weavers felt they had earned their place in musical history, but cannot recall that we ever discussed it. From the perspective of a twenty-five-year-old, they were acting old and couldn't seem to deal with the new material or each other. At the time, my focus was so narrow that I didn't wonder what the others felt about anything beyond rehearsals and performance. A couple of times, I asked why we weren't developing new material but quickly dropped the issue. From a musical standpoint, the Weavers felt comfortable with fairly simple lyrics and verse-chorus types of musical forms mixed with very close harmonies. There were modest exceptions to this formula—like "Darlin' Corey"—but they were rare. The newest music, like Dylan's poetry, stretched the limits in all directions and tended to be even more personal and reflective, concepts the Weavers seemed slow to grasp and incorporate into their music. It was as if they had bought into a certain folk image; that image was so firmly implanted that it left little room for growth. As I reflect on this now, I suppose I missed the point altogether. The Weavers were just plain tired.

By 1964, folk music in its commercial form was boring me to death. While it had been a major inspiration in my musical experience, it certainly wasn't my only interest. However, I was a long way from finding my own voice. I searched everywhere, turning to other influences like John Cage, Stockhausen, Boulez, a Brazilian by the name of Antonio Carlos Jobim, and Middle Eastern music.

Shortly after the Weavers broke up, I formed a duo with Bonnie Dobson. I loved her lyricism, personality, and richly-textured alto voice. We introduced a mix of traditional songs with jazz harmonies and rewritten lines. After a brief time, it was apparent that the folk idiom wasn't terribly tolerant of our musical embellishments; as a team, we did not have the industry backing to survive. We split in the spring of 1964, and I left New York to get involved in other aspects of music and recording. Folk music had reached a dead end for me.

and weep for their sins,

Detroit

By the mid-sixties, new audio technologies, such as multi-track recorders and signal-processing gear, were quickly becoming the production tools I could only dream about. Fascinated by the possibilities, I went back to Detroit and worked as a freelancer for several months at Motown; I did some producing and arranging, played guitar, and tested new studio skills. As it happened, I was one of only a handful of Caucasians working there. Our positions were always a bit tenuous. Berry Gordy's entire family worked for the company, and his allegiance to kin and friends came first. I admired his loyalty even if it didn't always work in my favor.

While living in Detroit, I met and married Denise, whose parents had been killed during the German occupation of France. Her father had died fighting for the Underground, and in 1944, Denise and her mother had been shipped from Paris to Auschwitz. By some miracle, Denise was saved by a French *flic* (policeman) and sent to live as a ward of the French state. She came to Detroit in the mid-fifties, learning the culture through television, movies, and a fair amount of reading. She had a sharp, if not dark, sense of humor, and her judgments about the world around her were like my mother's. However, throughout our marriage, Denise refused to work, saying, "Why should I work when you make so much money doing so little?" This forced me to work long and hard hours because I felt obligated to support her.

Unfortunately, it was a bad winter in the Midwest that season. Everything came to a standstill, including my freelance stint at Motown. I wanted to go to the West Coast, but Berry Gordy wouldn't send me. Having no other real prospects except for working in the family's business, I headed west, newly-married, with less than $200 to my name, and entirely prepared to work as a studio musician in Hollywood. With the promise of a job as staff music composer at Hanna-Barbera, the cartoon production company famous for "The Flintstones," I thought we would at least have a working income.

California

By the time I arrived, Hanna-Barbera had changed management, leaving me without a job after all. With a little hustling, I managed to convince a few producers to allow me to play studio guitar, mostly on television and radio commercial sessions. Then, a radio station in Santa Ana hired me to write ad copy and the music for its station identifications. It wasn't long before I was fired for my peculiar mix of religion, politics, and humor (which, according to the program director, who became particularly upset with me when I questioned why the station was still flying an American flag with forty-eight stars, was not the type of mix appropriate for the station), and because the station manager was always coming on to my wife. Without losing much sleep over the decision, Denise and I loaded up the VW and headed north to San Francisco.

In late 1965, I enrolled in the Tape Music Center at Mills College in Oakland where Karlheinz Stockhausen, a leading European composer of avant-garde music, was giving a series of lectures and workshops. Pauline Oliveros was also there, teaching early modular synthesizer. As I began to work with the newly developed modular electronic instruments and saw what some composers were doing with them, I found myself completely captivated. It was quite liberating to be able to create any number of complex rhythms and timbres and to discover, mostly by trial and error, whole new ways of expressing audio performances.

By 1966, I had begun to study electronic music seriously. It became immediately apparent to me, mostly because of our culture's affinity to technology, that this medium would be the next strong influence in studio production. For me, Bob Dylan's transition to electronics at the 1965 Newport Folk Festival opened up many possibilities for what was to come. His performance elated me. By this time, my own work in folk music was already becoming a peripheral part of my musical development. I was becoming more and more interested in a wider variety of styles and forms of music.

They do not make me sick

While studying electronic music at Mills College, I read an article about a man in New York who had been paid $35,000 for seven seconds of music for an American Express commercial. Five thousand dollars a second for six notes! Impulsively, I bought an airplane ticket and found myself heading east to meet this composer.

Eric Siday had purchased one of Robert Moog's first prototype modular instruments and had used it to create the commercial spot. During our meeting, Siday tried to recreate the commercial but was having technical difficulties, which he said were not unusual. As we talked, I couldn't take my gaze off the synthesizer—all six feet of it mounted on a table. It was so simple to operate that I was absolutely convinced I was seeing the future of media music unfolding before me.

Back at Mills, I told my teachers and colleagues what I had found but couldn't generate much enthusiasm. They were unimpressed by instruments that humans could easily control by methods that smacked of conventional keyboards. The academics had determined that the machine itself should generate random sounds which, by the composer's choice of inclusion or not, would ultimately be considered finished compositions.

Throughout this time in the Bay Area, I had a job as an account executive for a Lake Tahoe gambling casino. Unfortunately, the agency ran out of money soon after I was hired. After a few weeks without paychecks, John B., a friend from the agency, and I decided to open our own business. We calculated what was owed us in back wages, then went downtown to the office to reckon the value of the furniture and a couple of typewriters. We rented a truck, loaded it with various items, left a note for our ex-boss, and opened up our own office in an old, shabby building in downtown San Francisco.

Naming our new enterprise Parasound, we had no idea what we would do for a living. We tried many things. Once, we invested in an antigravity device. A black box appeared at our doorstep one evening, chaperoned by a down-and-out, acne-faced kid in his early twenties. Inside the box was a rotating arm mounted on a jury-rigged chassis that rotated around a fixed axis. When in motion, it was supposed to render the box and its contents weightless. However, when he set the spinner in motion, it went out of control, and parts flew all over the room; a valuable ceramic sculpture and some good dishes were destroyed in the process.

At that particular moment in our career, we were cynically convinced that print advertising was where it was at. The main goal of print advertising was to capture readership by offering short and simple, no-more-than-eighth-grade-reading-level messages that engaged the consumer long enough to convince them to buy the advertised product. John had earned his Ph.D. in communications and therefore knew intimately all of the possibilities. However, we thought up a venue for advertising that had been overlooked. For several weeks, we stood in lavatories, ostensibly washing our hands, but actually running a time clock on the average length of time men spent in stalls. It's a wonder we weren't arrested for loitering. After accumulating enough data, we calculated that each person spent at least a full minute in a stall. It didn't take much to see that an advertiser would receive 100 percent readership for a guaranteed period of time wherever their message was plastered on the inside of bathroom stall doors. Our next goal was to sell the concept, which we called LavaCard.

Ready to make our mark on the advertising world, we contacted Donnelly Outdoor Sign Company and forwarded a written proposal to the vice president of marketing. The proposal included all of our data and our plan for test-marketing the idea in gas stations along Route 66. When we called to arrange a meeting, the vice president picked up the phone and said, "This is the most scatological and deranged idea we've ever received, and I never want to hear your names again. Ever!"

With the twenty-three dollars we had left in our business account, John and I went out to Bay Meadows and bet it all on a horse. We're still waiting for it to finish.

———

One day while sitting in the office, desperately thinking of ways to earn some money before my credit cards were fully charged, I received a call from Jac Holzman, then president of Elektra Records. He had heard that I was working with synthesizers and asked if I knew Paul Beaver. I told Holzman that I had never actually met Paul, but I had heard about his work on "B" sci-fi movies and had seen him once on a film soundstage performing his magic. Holzman arranged for Paul to come north for a meeting because Elektra was considering commissioning an album that would be the first one to combine synthesizer and traditional orchestra for a piece based on some New Age gobbledygook about the Zodiac. Within an hour of meeting, Paul and I established an immediate and close rapport with one another and, over time, became unlikely but close friends.

Paul was a shy and quiet man who had grown up in rural Ohio. Extremely conservative, he wore a wide-lapel, double-breasted, blue serge suit wherever he went, on all but the hottest days in Los Angeles. There was always a sprinkling of dandruff on his shoulders and a small

Republican Party elephant adorning his left lapel. He described himself as politically to the right of John Ashbrook, an avid Scientologist, and bisexual. He tried only once to get me involved in all these scenes. He brought them up for discussion all at the same time, and we had what was to be our only intense disagreement; none of the issues was ever discussed again in my presence. But he did invite me to spaceship gatherings on the lower slopes of Mount Shasta, where he was certain that one of the seven refueling stops of interstellar vehicles was located. He'd also tell me stories of his wandering alone and naked around the mountain—only in the heat of summer when it was comfortable enough to do this, of course—trying to find the entrances for the spaceships. He claimed to have seen them. I listened to his detailed descriptions of these galactic happenings, but somehow my curiosity was never aroused enough to investigate.

Not long after our first meeting, Paul and I visited Robert Moog at his small factory near Ithaca, New York. We were concerned that his synthesizer would not be able to maintain stability of tunings and other key features. Undaunted, Moog placed a synthesizer on a three-foot high table and pushed it over the edge where it fell to the floor with a terrific thud. "That's my bench test," he chuckled as we looked on in horror. Then he plugged it in and let us try it. It worked! We bought one of the first models, pooling our life savings of $7,500 each to make the purchase. We did not know then what a struggle it would be to get people in the music industry to believe that this extraordinary electronic instrument was viable.

During the mid-sixties, Paul had purchased a run-down warehouse near downtown Los Angeles where he stored his arcane equipment (like the vintage theramin used to craft sci-fi's favorite *wee-ooh* sounds) and set up a small studio. It was in the midst of this controlled chaos that we plugged in our Moog synthesizer and began to explore our new musical voice. In the beginning, we had little money and were loaded with debt. I often slept on the floor under the long table upon which we had set up the synthesizer. Sometimes we bought small packages of pasta and cooked it on an electric burner in the bathroom for lunch, re-warming what was left over for dinner.

Because the instrument was so new, it had no history and there were no skilled synthesists to whom we could turn for advice or camaraderie. There was only a lot of conjecture and theory, and little of it applied to what we wanted to accomplish with our evolving knowledge. In many ways, we were like kids again, sometimes working for thirty-hour stretches to master a new technique or to create a new sound before collapsing from fatigue. While Paul immediately understood the language of the instrument, I was a much slower learner. He was very patient and would explain every detail of what he understood, sometimes over and over. Whenever we began the process of trying to learn a particular task, I would record his every word on cassette, then transcribe it later to see if it made sense to me. By May 1967, I had a complete set of notes on modular synthesizer techniques and acoustic principles.

Every time I learned a new skill or we had a musical revelation, I would make an appointment with a record or television producer and encourage them to try the synthesizer on their new projects. I always brought a tape demonstrating the sample we had just recorded. This went on for well over a year without much luck. The closest we came to a possible job was from a small label producer who said, "If you guys can do a cover of 'Monday, Monday,' maybe we can talk." We did a demo that was actually quite good, but the producer got fired, and we didn't get the contract.

Meanwhile, Holzman was the only person who was convinced that our technology would work; he had the foresight to feature it in his *Zodiac* album project. As part of the process, he envisioned an opportunity to include the synthesizer as an element of orchestration and to feature its use as a marketing tool. In late April 1967, a traditional live orchestra and our synthesizer combined for the first time in Hollywood at Western Recorders on Sunset Boulevard, and the *Zodiac* album was produced on Elektra using the Moog.

Despite the release of our album, I was still unable to interest anyone from the music community, commercial radio, or television production. Our *Zodiac* work with Elektra did not generate as much publicity as we had hoped. Furthermore, Walter Carlos's *Switched on Bach* was seen by most as a fluke, no matter how popular it may have been. Although we were nearly broke from our investment in equipment, Paul and I decided to try one last time to make a go of it.

discussing their duty to God,

A couple of months later, I found myself sitting next to Holzman on a flight from Los Angeles to Monterey. Using the last of our savings, Paul and I were going to demonstrate the synthesizer in a small booth at the Monterey Pops Festival. During the flight, I explained to Holzman that we had notes from our learning sessions on the Moog and showed him an outline of what we had done. Holzman suggested that we create a guide to electronic music for his Nonesuch label that would feature recorded samples of the raw sounds, descriptions of how they could be combined (synthesized) into new timbres, and a detailed booklet summarizing the techniques and rationale behind the product. Holzman offered us a $2,000 advance for our work and a small royalty. (For artists other than the Doors, Judy Collins, or Carly Simon, Holzman was not known for his spirit of generosity.) Paul and I saw this as a chance to demonstrate the potential of the technology. And two kilobucks was at least something. But first we needed to survive the Festival.

The booth was small. The few hundred dollars we were able to pool together got us a large folding table, a rented amplifier, and a cheap pair of headphones. At first, no one came, but little by little, individuals would arrive at our tiny 8 x 10 cubicle and queue up to lay their hands on the keyboard controllers we had programmed. We synthesized crashing waves, thunder and rain, and different instrumental sounds, depending on what we knew of the artists' taste. Paul would synthesize a Hammond B-3, trumpet, or string sound. I would set up a pattern on the sequencer that would play extended rhythm and melody lines through a tape delay unit then called an Echoplex, which provided a unique repeat or echo of the sound we had patched. The crowd was captivated, as it was generally stoned. It was also, thankfully, very well-heeled thanks to the generosity of CBS, RCA, and Capitol Records, who were literally fighting with each other to contract the talent represented in the Festival showcase.

By the second afternoon, the traffic jam in the aisle in front of our space became so large that security guards had to control the flow of people to and from our area! After a year of almost no work, we returned to Los Angeles a week later to find ourselves on-call in the studio, working at double scale, sixty to eighty hours a week, on major feature films and many hit albums with major groups. We actually had to buy a second synthesizer to cover our numerous projects. For the first time, we began to make a good living. However, I hated the traffic and the smog in Los Angeles, and I refused to move south, preferring instead to commute from San Francisco several times a week.

While working madly on these projects, Paul and I began to create the electronic music guide for Holzman. The main question we had to resolve was how, and whether, electronic media altered the definition of music, and whether the Western academic models were too restrictive. We felt they were, and we set about to add new information to the existing paradigms.

Both Paul and I came from the fringes of different traditions. Although we were both classically trained musicians and understood the current popular music styles, our main thoughts centered around whether or not the music—any music—sounded true to its form, medium, and roots, and whether this made it sound convincing.

Academia had been trying to define ethnomusicology and its various frontiers ever since I could remember. (To my mind, it has come no closer to success at the end of the twentieth century than it was at the beginning. Even so, music of the late twentieth century encompasses a much broader scope of inquiry now than what was allowed thirty years ago. There are aspects commonly covered today that would have caused a major riot if the issues had been brought up for inclusion then.) After helping to introduce the synthesizer as a viable instrument and writing the original *Nonesuch Guide to Electronic Music* (1968), Paul Beaver and I presented a new definition of music, limiting it to three words. Quite simply: control of sound.

The *Nonesuch Guide to Electronic Music* took four months to complete. All of the recording was done at our studio in Los Angeles. It was an agonizing and grueling process, and we threw out several different versions of the music because it was simply not what we wished to release. I wrote and typed the detailed manuscript for the album booklet, which explained acoustics, analog synthesis of sound, and audio terms, at the kitchen table in my small apartment in San Francisco. As Paul learned the intricacies of the synthesizer, he would call me into the studio and offer convoluted explanations of what he was doing and why. Completely unfamiliar with and intimidated by technology, I paid careful attention to his every word and move. From our first meeting, I questioned and recorded everything for later review. With the tapes from those sessions, I began to transcribe the text for the *Guide*, finally finding some useful outlet for my extensive notes. When concepts weren't clear, I went back to our studio for yet another session with Paul so that I could fully grasp and explain them. As a result, I not only finished something original, but I had also learned valuable knowledge about acoustics and the synthesis of sound.

The night I finished the *Guide,* I cried from relief and the sheer joy of personal accomplishment. Whereas none of my other work felt truly original or particularly creative, this was the first time I had completed a task that I alone had initiated. It simply felt wonderful and gratifying. The only other time in my life that I have felt a similar sense of pride was, fifteen years later, when I formulated the idea of *biophonies*—the ways in which animals in any natural habitat vocalize as an orchestra. For the first time, I was elated by the certainty that I had done good work that might be helpful to others. By the time the *Guide* was completed and the master tapes given to Elektra/Nonesuch, Paul and I had spent over $10,000 of our own money on the project in production costs alone—money we were never to recover even though the album was on the Billboard charts for twenty-six weeks.

Not one is dissatisfied...

Soon after the release of the *Nonesuch Guide*, Limelight Records, a subsidiary of Mercury, signed us to their label, and we recorded an album called *Ragnarök* (Mercury Records, 1968). With the help of Van Dyke Parks, we began the long process of turning the synthesizer into an instrument of musical expression—one with a voice all its own. Intrigued by the musical possibilities, our new friend, George Martin, the elegant arranger/producer genius behind the Beatles, bought an instrument from us and agreed to write liner notes for the album jacket. Although the album and the record company were largely unsuccessful, *Ragnarök* served as a major breakthrough for many recording techniques we were to use on future projects. Our growing enterprise, however, was not without many setbacks.

The main problem we experienced in the studio was the producers' request that we synthesize the sounds of strings, horns on demand, and other traditional instruments. One day, when we were working on a film soundstage where a feature was being scored, we filled in for some string players who were late because of another session across town that had run into overtime. At the end of the session, the union contractor from the American Federation of

Musicians (AFM) Los Angeles Local 47 demanded our presence at the office for what he described as a "little discussion." Paul and I showed up at the AFM offices late in the afternoon and were seated at a conference table surrounded by an intimidating group of serious-looking men. We were armed with a small cassette recorder, which we placed in the middle of the table in clear view of the others. One of the union officers began the discussion, informing us that we had violated an unwritten law that prevented any electronic technology from replacing other musicians. Prepared for the argument, Paul cited the Hammond Organ case of the late 1930s, when many of the old instruments used in solo lounge acts had a "rhythm" or drum machine that established a beat to which the organist performed. He reminded them that the union had once tried to ban its use, but had lost the restraint-of-trade issue in the U.S. Court of Appeals nearly thirty years before. Unmoved, the AFM threatened to shut us down unless we promised never again to try to emulate string or horn sounds, thereby replacing other musicians. When we asked them how they described our studio performance if *we* weren't musicians, they were silent. We then asked them to put their threat in writing, which they promptly did.

We took the tape and document directly to our attorney, who promptly called the president of AFM International in New York and informed him that unless the issue was dropped, Beaver and Krause would file a $500 million restraint-of-trade lawsuit against the union based on the merits of the Hammond case. Faced with litigation and some bad press, the AFM dropped their threat, and although we continued to hear grumblings about synthesizers replacing musicians, we were never again restricted from synthesizing strings or horns or anything else. Much to our surprise, the little publicity we got brought us even more work.

Although Paul and I had been appointed sales agents for Moog, we were largely unconcerned about the repercussions of our seminars and sales to other artists. We were so busy then that we actively welcomed the competition we were creating. For us, the main problem was exhaustion. Not only were we working steadily, but we also gave synthesizer classes and tutored individuals at night. Some of those we worked with included Elmer Bernstein, George Martin, Dave Grusin, George Harrison, The Beach Boys, Van Morrison, and Frank Zappa, among others. Recording sessions with most of these artists were generally short. In most cases, we did not spend more than a few hours performing on a particular song and had little interaction with the artist beyond the work at hand.

As a result of the success of the *Nonesuch Guide* and the extensive film work we were doing, we connected with a whole new group of exciting talent. Among them were Randy Newman and Van Dyke Parks. They were what Warner Brothers called "experimental" artists during the golden era of American pop music, when the record companies tended to be run by people with vision and courage rather than the MBAs who began to take over in the late seventies. Van Dyke and Randy were instrumental in bringing us to the attention of Joe Smith, then the president of Warner Brothers Records. We worked out the terms of a contract with Smith for a series of albums that would ultimately change the course of my life. During the sketches of the first concept, I thought often of my parents, who had inadvertently brought me to the edge of this pilgrimage in spite of themselves and their fears.

With our new Warner Brothers contract in hand, Paul and I were sitting in our studio one fall day in 1968 when Van Dyke Parks came by to chat. Paul and I had been talking about the theme of our next album and were remarking that the music we were hearing as a result of the glut of synthesizer recordings was already becoming tedious. As synthesizer studio musicians much in demand, we had little time for work of our own. Even so, we were being asked more frequently to replicate our own sounds or the sounds we had created for artists like Stevie Wonder, the Byrds, or the Doors. It was becoming clear that we had to take a different creative tack.

Van Dyke suggested that we do something on *ecology*—a new word for us, but one that would have an impact on our lives much sooner than we thought. With all of the new, more compact technologies, he urged us to try recording material in natural environments and use it as a compositional element in our music. In that way, he suggested, we could use our art to address the need to preserve habitats and use the sounds as a new source of music for our craft. I admit that this idea, at first, was not terribly intriguing. Both Paul and I had always lived in cities, and we knew nothing about field recording besides the small amount of ambient sound or effects we created for film. But Paul had a small Uher recorder and a couple of decent mics. I took the equipment home with me and began to experiment. In the meantime, we decided that our album would be called *In a Wild Sanctuary*, which was inspired by a line from the late nineteenth century American author, Ellen Glasgow: "Preserve, within a wild sanctuary, an inaccessible valley of reveries."

San Francisco

With a portable recorder slung over my shoulder and a pair of stereo mics in hand, I drove to what I then considered a natural habitat—Muir Woods—located north of San Francisco in Marin County. Aside from the noise of light aircraft and distant traffic, there was not a creature sound to be heard. Of course, it didn't immediately occur to me that I was trying to record in late fall, when most of the birds and other animals were either absent or fairly silent. Also, redwood habitats, compared to other types of habitats, are not as aurally robust. Undaunted, I continued the search. I visited the ocean and recorded waves. I hiked to a nearby stream and recorded the sound of trickling water. I went to the beach by Fisherman's Wharf to capture people at play by the water's edge, and then I visited the zoo.

Just to hear the habitats transformed through stereo headphones at each site had a powerful impact on me. The sounds were resplendent. Amplified and more vivid then those we generally hear, the sounds had a feeling of space that was vastly expanded and lustrous. I recorded for hours, riveted by what I *thought* I was hearing. However, when I returned to my studio and tried playing back my field recordings, I was completely horrified. To my great disappointment, almost none of the tracks sounded like what I remembered hearing only a few hours before. The ocean waves sounded diminished and distant. The stream sounded like constant static. The redwood forest sounds were composed mostly of hiss—produced by a combination of the audio tape and noise introduced by the electronics of the recorder—and a few indistinct bird calls. Except for the sounds at Fisherman's Wharf, nothing was as I had heard. The illusion and magic of the moment was completely lost, and I had no idea why. I began to think of our experience in film sound and remembered that the *effect,* or illusion of sound, is much more important to the human ear than the sound's original source.

As it happened, our stream sound on *In a Wild Sanctuary* was ultimately created by placing a pair of mics in a toilet bowl and letting the water run so that the effect sounded like a stream. We never got the ocean waves right so we synthesized them, just as we did the thunder. The bird sounds had to wait until mating time in the spring of '69. The zoo sounds required many more visits as well.

During the six months it took us to orchestrate *In a Wild Sanctuary,* we tried many different ways to fold natural sound recordings into our music. Late one evening, I walked through San Francisco's Nob Hill neighborhood, hoping to catch some environmental sound that would inspire music. The rhythmic pulse of the underground cables that power the cable cars caught my attention. As I walked into the middle of the street to place my mics in the cable slots, a man came up to me from the opposite side of the street and asked what I was doing. He introduced himself as Frank Oppenheimer, founder of the Exploratorium (he later informed me that he was the brother of the late J. Robert). He watched, completely absorbed, as I recorded samples of the cable rhythms. When I finished, we went to a nearby coffee shop to chat. I told him about our idea to use sound to convey aspects of the natural environments that were disappearing everywhere. He, in turn, told me about his experiences trying to get Exploratorium board members to listen to his ideas about how to relate the wonders of nature. "Use your cable recordings to symbolize the ways in which Western industry has depleted our resources," he offered. "The sounds of pure nature are so rare now, that people don't even recognize environments when they hear the recordings." Most of his efforts, he said, had fallen on deaf ears. When we parted for the evening, he gripped my hand warmly and expressed the hope that Paul and I would somehow be more successful.

not one is demented with the mania of owning things,

In a Wild Sanctuary, finished late in the spring of 1969, introduced many new elements into the field of music and music synthesis. It was the first time unaltered natural sound had been directly used as a component of orchestration, a technique I would further develop in natural sound sculptures. Another feature we introduced on the album was the method used in a tune called "Spaced." Conceptually, the music begins with the chaos of simulated wooden wind chimes mixed with a flute-like obbligato that has the spatial effect of moving around the listener's head as it is performing. Toward the end of this section a single note, G, is introduced and heard from a distance. Gradually, as it is brought closer in perspective to the listener, it splits into eight parts with each note traveling through a long glissando, while, at the same time, getting closer and closer to the listener until it finally resolves into an eight-note D-major chord. That piece was knocked off by radio stations for their identifications, a major automobile company for its commercials, and a well-established Northern California film company that has used a remarkably similar concept as a trailer for their cinema audio system for years. Their film company composer failed to disguise this "coincidence," beginning his iteration on the same note and resolving it on precisely the same D-major chord. (Despite the fact that we have a copyright on the music and had recorded it some fourteen years prior to their unlicensed use, our friendly local film company continues to claim that it originated the performance, even though our version had been distributed worldwide for well over a decade.)

Our rendition of "Walking Green Algae Blues," featuring Howard Roberts on guitar and Paul on the Hammond organ, was an environmental lament dedicated to Frank Oppenheimer. That tune, like others on the album, expressed a strong anti-war and environmental sentiment, something Paul initially felt uncomfortable with because of his rather conservative political leanings. It didn't take long to convince him that speaking out through our music was the right action. While on a trip to Lausanne, Switzerland, in the early seventies, I discovered that Daniel Cohn-Bendit, the leader of the French student uprising in 1968, had adopted the tune as the anthem for his new Green Party that he was forming in Germany. Paul found these acknowledgments of our work both appalling and amusing. On the one hand, he expressed delight when our music found an audience. Yet he saw Cohn-Bendit's endorsement as embarrassing since he would subsequently have to defend our work when the press or audience members asked questions about it. Finally, the album was the first recording to be encoded in quadraphonic and surround sound in all available playback formats.

In a Wild Sanctuary was an enormous critical success but only a moderate commercial one. We were able to get a great deal of film scoring and studio work in Hollywood, New York, and London as a result. More than all of the financial rewards, however, the process of recording the album left me with a sense of dedication and direction that completely altered my future work.

Most importantly, I discovered that being outdoors and recording could be complementary endeavors. Each time I went further afield, I found myself energized and inspired by what I heard and experienced. Also, I became less terrified and began to find comfort working alone in remote areas of what I've come to know as the wild natural—isolated habitats that still exist more or less in their wild, natural state. I often found myself daydreaming about doing nothing but being outdoors, recording for the rest of my life. The thought of working in an office or studio gnawed at me, and I began to have nightmares about session work, where Paul and I would frequently waste our time waiting for self-indulgent artists to sober up and get their act together.

I took *In a Wild Sanctuary* very much to heart as a creative and expressive center for our work, and as a *raison d'être* for working in a quiet place with fresh air and a place where I could learn about the disappearing wildness around me. Every time I thought about the ways in which I wanted to put these types of natural sound albums together, I felt calmer and more focused. But at the same time, I had bought into a lifestyle "demented with the mania of owning things" that demanded quite different standards. Because of my troubled marriage to Denise, I wasn't quite ready to give up this lifestyle, even though conflicting signals were becoming stronger with each passing day.

Not one kneels to another nor to his kind

Late one fall night in 1968, George Harrison phoned me at home and asked if I would come to London and bring a Moog synthesizer with me. I had already sold one to George Martin and to Mick Jagger. A month earlier, Harrison had asked me to play synthesizer on his Jackie Lomax album production at Armin Steiner's Sound Recorders in Hollywood. After the session was wrapped up, Harrison asked me to stay behind and demonstrate the Moog set-ups I had used on the session as well as other possible sounds. It was already quite late, around 3:00 A.M., and I had flown in from San Francisco early the previous day. In my exhausted state, I didn't notice that he had ordered the engineer to keep a tape machine rolling. Had I been aware that he was recording my demonstration, I would have never shown examples of what Paul and I were considering for our next album, which was to be *Gandharva*. As I showed him the settings and gave some performance examples, Harrison seemed impressed with the possibilities. I had no idea at the time exactly how impressed he was.

At the end of the demonstration, he asked me when he could get a Moog III delivered to London. I told him that he could have it thirty days after we got a 50 percent deposit. He reminded me that he was, after all, a Beatle, and the Apple Music Organization generally didn't give deposits. In a calm voice and looking him straight in the eye, I responded that as soon as I received a deposit check from Apple and it cleared the bank, a synthesizer would be on its way within a month. He asked if we could move up the schedule for him—again, because he was a Beatle. I told him that there were no exceptions.

After a couple of months, I got a call from George, asking where his synthesizer was. Feeling that I was speaking with a total idiot, I once again repeated the terms. He agreed, then asked if I would personally travel with the Moog to London to help clear customs and to teach him how to operate the machine. I said that I would, as long as he paid for my expenses and time, thinking that it would be wonderful to meet the other members of the group. I had heard rumors of their impending split and wanted to experience the inner circle before its demise.

Early in January 1969, another call came from Harrison, telling me that a deposit had been sent and that I should arrange to come over to London to work with him. (He never asked if it was convenient, or possible, or if the timing was right; he just said, "arrange to come.") He said that he would pay for my expenses but nothing for my time. "You're selling the bloody things!" he reminded me. "Now show me how to play it!" He had a point.

A first class ticket arrived in the mail, which I immediately cashed in for two coach tickets so that my wife could accompany me. The Friday before we left, I checked with Harrison to confirm the trip. The Apple office verified all the arrangements.

Seated in the aisle and middle seats in the first row behind the first class bulkhead of an old 707, we had a clear view of the first class cabin. As the plane pulled away from the gate, a female passenger in first class jumped up and began to rip off her clothes screaming,

"The plane's going to crash! Everyone get off 'cause the plane's going to crash!"

Robert Mitchum, who was apparently sitting a row behind her, calmly got up and wrapped a blanket around the woman as the plane returned to the gate so that the flight attendants could get her off the flight. As it turned out, this was Dory Previn in the throes of her breakup with her conductor-husband, André, which subsequently led to the mental breakdown she would later write about. The trip began unpleasantly and never varied.

London

Apple had booked us into the Dorchester Hotel. It was within walking distance of the office, and so, after settling in, I walked over to the Apple shrine to find out what was happening. The approach from the street looked more like a circus, with lots of kids milling about in different trendy costumes, gawking at whomever entered the hallowed gates. When I went into the office, I was greeted by the first security battalion with an air of incredible snottiness and indifference. No one seemed to know that I was expected—even though they had ordered the synthesizer, sent me a ticket, and arranged for my stay in one of the better hotels in town on their tab. Finally, someone volunteered that Harrison had his tonsils removed the previous Friday (the day I called to confirm the trip) and would be out of commission for about a week. I'd have to cool it, they told me. They would call when George was ready.

I hadn't planned to stay in London more than a week to work with Harrison and felt in my gut that this was going to turn into a major ordeal. Having finally located Harrison's assistant, I told him that I could be reached in Paris at a particular hotel and he should call me when Harrison was ready. I also gave the forwarding number to the Beatle's business manager, a couple of the secretaries, and to the concierge of the Dorchester. Figuring I'd covered my bases, Denise and I went to Paris.

Several days passed; I don't remember how many. Every couple of days I would call the Apple office to see if there was any news. It was always the same, "He'll call when he's ready." Finally, after about a week, a call came from the office. "Where the fuck have you been!?" a voice screamed from the other end. "George has been sitting around waiting for you for days! Why aren't you where you're supposed to be? And furthermore, we haven't been able to get the synthesizer out of customs, and we need help because they can't define what the bloody thing is, and we sure as bloody hell don't want to pay the tax they want to charge us!"

Completely caught off-guard, I told the woman on the end to shove her attitude where the sun don't shine and to call me back when she got it straightened out. Then I hung up. When she called back apologetically, I outlined in clear terms what I required if they wanted my help with anything and told the assistant that I would return to London in a couple of days.

Meeting our flight at Heathrow, the Apple folks drove us directly to British customs where the instrument was still being held. I had asked the office to send an amplifier to the airport with the driver so that we could play the synthesizer live. That suggestion saved the day. From customs' perspective, the synthesizer was still an uncategorized or miscellaneous electronic device. The import duty would therefore be some outrageous sum of 60 or 70 percent. However, if it was an electronic organ, the duty fell below 10 percent—an enormous savings on a $15,000 instrument. The agent allowed me to unpack the synthesizer and demonstrate it to him. I plugged it into the amplifier, patched a few oscillators, quickly synthesized a Hammond B-3 organ sound, and proceeded to play a couple of musical lines. Satisfied that it was only an electronic organ, he allowed Apple to pay the requisite tax and let the instrument into the country.

Late in the afternoon, two cars came to the hotel to take me and my wife, separately, to Harrison's house in Esher, a suburb outside of London. Its location was so obscure that the driver was provided with a radio telephone so that he could be "talked" through the maze of small streets to get to the house. In the light of the headlights, the house looked like a low-lying, one-story, suburban ranch-style residence that would look more in place somewhere around Houston. Its only distinguishing mark was a garage door outrageously decorated with a psychedelic graphic all but obscured by the Mercedes parked in front. Harrison's wife, Patty, answered the door and asked if we would like something to eat. We were ushered into the kitchen where George and Patty were making a large salad. "We're vegetarians, you know. We don't eat meat and don't like to use products from dead animals," he said, offering the compulsory joint and escorting me into the living room. He promptly directed us to sit on a fifteen-foot long leather couch; I didn't bother to ask where the leather for the couch came from.

In one corner of the living room, there was an uncrated multi-track tape recorder and a two-track machine with a tape cued up and ready to play. The Moog synthesizer had been set up along the opposite wall facing the leather couch. Any conversation was interrupted by phone calls and people dropping by the house to ask George if he wanted to buy this Mercedes or that Ferrari. Harrison seemed greatly distracted by all the activity while, at the same time, reveling in the commotion. Finally, things calmed down for a while and Harrison returned to the room. "Before we get started," he said, "I want to play something for you that I did on a synthesizer. Apple will release it in the next few months. It's my first electronic piece done with a little help from my cats."

He hit the "play" button on the recorder. At first I didn't recognize the material. However, little by little I became increasingly uncomfortable, knowing that I had heard this performance before. After a few more minutes I realized that the recording was taken from the Lomax demo session I had played for Harrison only a few months earlier.

I finally mustered my courage and said, "George, this is my music. Why is it on this tape and why are you representing it as yours?"

"Don't worry," he answered, "I've edited it and if it sells, I'll send you a couple of quid."

"Wait a minute, George, you never asked me if you could use this material." I said. "We need to talk about it." At which point he got red in the face and began to get pissed.

"You're coming on like you're Jimi Hendrix," he said, his voice rising in pitch and volume. "When Ravi Shankar comes to my house, he's humble." Then, as if not to be undone by this American upstart, he screamed his most famous line, "Trust me, I'm a Beatle!"

I quietly got up, put on my coat, and asked him to order me a car because I'd had enough and was going home. As I waited for my ride, he had the audacity to ask me if I would show him how to set up a bagpipe sound. Without saying a word, I patched one for him and left thinking that all he had to do was to stick the chanter up his butt—and blow.

George Harrison's album, *Electronic Music,* was released some months later. But not before I had it recalled and ordered my name taken off the cover. I didn't have the money or energy to sue him. The proper retribution would have to wait for someone more courageous and less intimidated by Harrison's tendencies to copy—like the person who wrote "My Sweet Lord" and chased George down until the matter was settled against Harrison. Rather then reprinting the album cover, Apple simply had my name silvered over. (If you can find one of the old issues of the album, hold it in the right light, and you can still faintly see my name right there—spelled incorrectly, of course.) Although I did get credit on the inside jacket, along with his cats, I never did receive a single "quid." Also, the son-of-a-bitch never did invite me back to his house so I could show him my "I'm-as-humble-as-Ravi-Shankar" act, which I've been practicing ever since.

I told the story to a reporter at *Rolling Stone*, but his editor refused to accept it because Harrison was their media hero of the moment. Instead, they ran a story about George shopping for shoes. They even refused to publish my letter to the editor describing what had transpired, although, with some pressure, they finally published a seriously edited form of it many months later. Mostly, at the time, I was astonished and confused by the difference between Harrison's image and what I experienced in the studio and at his home. His refusal to acknowledge where he got the material left me sad and enraged, but also feeling powerless. And certainly, a little wiser and more cynical. I try to understand greed and the endless need for power, but to this day, I cannot accept that it is the only way some people feel the need to act toward one another.

The Harrison experience was disappointing because I had different expectations of what our relationship would be and could have been. By that time, I was known as a talented synthesist, an excellent programmer, and could have been very helpful if I had been treated better. However, I had much more important things to think about—like my new project with Paul that would include jazz immortals and heroes like Gerry Mulligan, Howard Roberts, Bud Shank, and ourselves, all in the same group. We had long thought about doing an album that spoke of noise in our environment, intentionally using a poorly recorded rock and roll cut at the beginning as an example of aural pollution, then gradually making the album quieter and more peaceful to the fading echo of the last lingering note at the end.

that lived thousands of years ago,

San Francisco

For years I had dreamed of putting together a major group of musicians to help Paul and me realize one of our more ambitious compositional ideas. Our big chance came as we were preparing to record *Gandharva*, our second album for Warner Brothers. With the budget provided by the record company, we were able to bring together many extraordinary artists such as Leroy Vinnegar, Mulligan, Mike Bloomfield, Shank, Roberts, and Gale Laughton.

To get a reverberation effect, we wanted to rent a decommissioned Nike missile silo located north of Sacramento. Our thought was to turn "swords" into music. But when we visited the site to test record, we accidentally dropped an expensive four-track recorder forty feet into the giant pit. Because of the local press about the Nike silo incident, we got many calls for alternative venues to record in. Offers of cisterns, churches, empty warehouses, the holds of cargo boats, and storm drains poured in. Then we were offered San Francisco's magnificent Grace Cathedral, the best venue of all.

Our idea was to present this progressive musical journey of "noise" to the ethereal, in what was to be the first live quadraphonic album ever produced. To avoid outside traffic noise, we rented the cathedral during the late evening and early morning hours. Mics were suspended everywhere throughout the space so that Mulligan and Shank could walk along the floor of the ninety-foot high nave as they played, adding a spatial dimension to their performances.

The effect certainly surpassed any chemical rapture I had ever experienced and was one of the best pieces of music Paul and I were to create. I was so enlivened by what we were writing and performing that four nights passed without my even noticing that I had not slept. Later, at our record release party in San Francisco, the Grateful Dead road crew became so captivated by the production that they donated their time and equipment, setting up the best stage system we had ever heard so that the album could be presented in its full spatial grandeur—the only time, I suspect, that it was ever heard in that form.

With the completion of *Gandharva*, Paul and I began looking for interesting new themes and novel ways to use the synthesizer and incorporate it into our music. From my experience with *In a Wild Sanctuary*, I knew that the recording of natural sounds would eventually be a full-time job if it was to be done well. From the album's completion, every spare moment I had was spent searching out locations to record these elusive sounds. The process of recording *In a Wild Sanctuary* gave me insight into several important difficulties we would continually face, including the extensive time needed to get good material because of noise, and certain critters who only vocalized at specific times, seasons, or under particular weather conditions.

Early on, this process also led me to seriously consider the relationship between natural environments and the music these habitats might inspire, particularly in cultures that lived in close contact with the land. My attention was diverted further and further afield until I found myself inexorably drawn to the Nez Perce Indians near Lewiston, Idaho, for some answers. What I discovered near the reservation was surprising.

Part II

Not one is respectable or industrious

Before the European migration to North America, Native Americans experienced natural sound as an outdoor symphony where all the creature voices performed as an integral part of an animal orchestra. The varied iterations of wind, rain, insects, birds, amphibians, and mammals during each season made up the fabric of their aural experience. This special combination of sounds not only helped define physical territories for each tribe, but also served to strongly influence their music. As their habitats became radically transformed by deforestation, agriculture, and urbanization, and with many tribes decimated by war and disease, numerous Native American families lost their direct source of sonic natural textures in a relatively short period of time. Where their music had always been directly related to the natural world before contact with Western culture, a profound breach was created as the wild natural became so deeply transformed, and this connection was all but lost. In some isolated areas of the planet, however, this fragile natural link still exists. Older forest-dwelling humans are still keenly aware of the impact of natural sound on the totality of their lives and integrate their knowledge of sounds into nearly every spiritual and non-spiritual aspect of their daily existence.

From the combined perspective of artist and naturalist, I have long been intrigued by the ways in which nighttime hunters from non-industrial societies use sound to determine the types, numbers, and condition of game (and other creatures) that are hundreds of meters away. In these cultures, it is astounding how closely their music reflects the complex rhythms, polyphonies, and sonic textures of the habitats where they live and hunt. Unlike these highly sophisticated groups, industrial societies are primarily visual cultures, no longer connected spiritually or aesthetically to the sounds of the natural wild. As a consequence, we've lost a certain aural acuity once central to the dynamic of our lives. This, of course, has had a profound impact on our understanding of the natural world, which we now experience as abstract and distorted. For me, the first glimpse into our ancient aural past began to unfold about thirty years ago.

Lake Wallowa. Northeast Oregon

I worked with the Nez Perce in Idaho and central Washington in the late sixties and early seventies, recording oral histories, music, and natural ambient sound. Many of the Elders, wishing to have their traditions preserved, generously permitted us to record their stories. These exchanges of family histories played an important role, establishing a mutual trust over a period of many months. One member we interviewed, tribal Elder Angus Wilson, suddenly became very pensive and quiet one afternoon when I told him, among other personal revelations, that I was a musician. "You white folks know nothing about music," he said, half-serious, half-teasing with a confrontation unusual in his culture. "But I'll teach you something about it if you want."

Early the next morning, we drove from Lewiston to Lake Wallowa, one of the many campsites in northeastern Oregon where Chief Joseph had lived and where the Nez Perce had lived and hunted for many centuries. Wilson led my colleague and me to the bank of a

Bernie, c. 1941, was drawn to sound at a young age.

Bernie's parents, Guilda and Sydney Krause, in Ann Arbor, Michigan, c. 1935.

Living in Boston, Bernie, c. 1962, set up an annual folk concert series.

Carnegie Hall Thursday Eve., May 2nd and Friday Eve., May 3rd, 1963

HAROLD LEVENTHAL

Presents

The Fifteenth Anniversary Concert

THE WEAVERS

ERIK DARLING   RONNIE GILBERT   LEE HAYS   FRED HELLERMAN
FRANK HAMILTON   PETE SEEGER
And BERNIE KRAUSE

Tonight marks an historic event, the celebration of the fifteenth anniversary of THE WEAVERS. The pioneering efforts and influence that this group has had on folk music in our country has resulted to a large extent in the great popularity and mass audience that folk music now enjoys.

Program continued on page 9

Program for the Weavers' 1964 Carnegie Hall Reunion concert.

L to R: Ronnie Gilbert, Eric Darling, Freddie Hellerman, and Lee Hays of the Weavers, c. 1960. *Photograph from Michael Ochs Archives, Venice, CA.*

Performing with Bonnie Dobson, 1964. *Photograph by David Mahill.*

Paul Beaver at San Francisco's Grace Cathedral, 1969. *Photograph by Graham Arlen, Oakland, CA.*

Taping *Gandharva* at Grace Cathedral, 1969. *Photograph by Graham Arlen, Oakland, CA.*

Saxophonist Gerry Mulligan at Grace Cathedral, 1969. *Photograph by Graham Arlen, Oakland, CA.*

Tribal Elder Angus Wilson of the Nez Perce, Lake Wallowa, northeastern Oregon, 1972. *Photograph by Robert Primes.*

Cheetah photographed during Kenya trip for the California Academy of Sciences, 1983. *Photograph by Bernie Krause.*

Recording a tortoise, Kenya, 1983.

Rescue efforts during Humphrey the Whale's return to the San Francisco Bay in 1989. *Photograph by Bernie Krause.*

Tom Wrubel, founder of The Nature Company, 1986. *Photograph courtesy of The Nature Company.*

An orang-utan near Camp Leakey, Borneo, 1991. *Photograph by Bernie Krause.*

Nick Nichols photographing the Virunga Mountains along the Rwanda-Zaire border, 1987. *Photograph by Bernie Krause.*

Recording silverback gorillas, Rwanda, 1987. *Photograph by Nick Nichols, Magnum Photos.*

Photos on the wall of Dian Fossey's cabin, Rwanda, 1987, two years after her murder. *Photograph by Nick Nichols, Magnum Photos.*

The gorilla graveyard near Dian Fossey's cabin, Rwanda, 1987. *Photograph by Bernie Krause.*

Recording insect larvae in a tidepool near Point Reyes, 1992. *Photograph by Fred Mertz.*

small stream, the east fork of the Wallowa River, and motioned for us to sit quietly on the ground. In the chilly October mountain air, we sat huddled in fetal positions, arms wrapped tightly to our sides, trying to keep ourselves warm for the better part of an hour. Every now and then, we glanced in the direction of Angus, who sat stoically and motionless about fifty feet upstream. For a long while, except for the calls of a few jays and ravens, we heard nothing. After what seemed like a long time, a slight breeze came from up the valley and began to stir the branches of the aspen and fir trees. Suddenly, the whole forest burst into a cathedral of sound! Like a huge pipe organ with all the stops out, a giant cacophonous chord echoed from everywhere throughout the valley. Angus, seeing the startled looks on our faces, walked slowly in our direction and said, "Do you know yet what makes the sound?"

"No," I said, shivering and irritated. "I haven't the slightest idea."

Without another word, he walked over to the bank of the stream and, kneeling low to the water's edge, pointed to the reeds that had been broken different lengths by wind and ice. Slipping a hunting knife from the leather sheath hanging at his belt, Angus cut one of the reeds at the waterline, whittled some holes, and, without tuning the instrument, brought the transformed reed to his lips and played a melody. After a long while, he stopped and said quietly, "This is how we learned our music."

Kenya

Ten years later, that chilly morning at Lake Wallowa with Angus Wilson came to mind again. I had been recording sounds in the forest, working long hours over many evenings, waiting for some grazing elephants to stop pulling up the trees around our tent and render some vocalizations. Exhausted, I experienced the early morning insect sounds and distant hyenas as a kind of dream in which they performed as an animal symphony. As this occurred, many thoughts came to me all at once. Through the haze of weariness, I gradually became conscious of the possibility that this wasn't a dream and recorded the ambience to see if I would feel the same way later when I revisited the moment on tape.

———

Since the end of the nineteenth century, researchers in the natural sciences have focused their work largely on the study of single creatures in order to understand an organism's connection to the whole environment. This is based on the assumption that isolated studies are always easier to observe and measure within the canons of pure and carefully considered academic terms—that once each part is understood, the whole can somehow be extrapolated. It is easier to impose controls on the study—the quantified results offer models that fit common expectations—at the expense of comprehensive knowledge. Indeed, even in my relatively new field of bio-acoustics (bio = life, acoustics = sound), when portable and professional quality tape recorders and microphones that could be used outdoors first emerged in the late sixties, field researchers enthusiastically taped single creature sounds and isolated individual animal vocalizations only to find that significant parts of the messages eluded them altogether. It is what Stephen Jay Gould calls "the invisibility of larger contexts caused by too much focus upon single items, otherwise known as missing the forest through the trees." ("Abolish the Recent," *Natural History*, May, 1991, pages 16-21.) Bearing this in mind, we are just now beginning to explore the important role ambient sound plays in our environment. Hearing the sounds in context with each other tells the creature story in a very different way. From my perspective, taking the voice of a single animal from a habitat and trying to understand it out of context is a little like trying to comprehend an elephant by examining only a single hair at the tip of its tail (before cloning, of course).

Our ancestors had intimate knowledge of what successfully drives many forest inhabitants today. It is the knowledge that in every biome of the wild natural, where the environment is still intact, a unique voice made up of the complex relationships between all vocal creatures is quite unequaled. All sound-producing organisms generate utterances that fit solely into their environment relative to other vocal or sound-creating organisms in that territory. These organisms, when vocalizing, produce niches measurable by time (rhythm) and frequency (pitch). Furthermore, they have evolved sound-generating communication mechanisms that create audio output complementary and relative to other noise-producing creatures and the particular acoustical properties of their respective habitats. From what I can tell, this phenomenon occurs in every type of habitat on the planet, marine and terrestrial. What is especially noteworthy is the way in which the acoustic niche changes as one moves short distances throughout a forest—even where vegetation and the geological features appear constant. While there are general or regional similarities, any subtle change in the mix of creatures changes the manner in which the niche articulates itself, thus defining territorial grids of many shapes and sizes that are often in a state of flux. These are vastly different perameters than the usual scientific grids of 100 square meters we were originally taught to use.

Figures 1 and 2 show simple and complex habitat ambient niches where consistent dark lines running horizontally across the page represent a unique mixture of insect voices occupying several "bands" of a 20–10,000 Hertz frequency spectrum in Figure 1, and a 20–20 kHz. spectrum in Figure 2. The darker the line, the greater the amplitude in that particular range. The short lines toward the bottom of the page in Figure 1 represent the low voice of a Zenaida dove (*Zenaida macroura*), a species of bird living in the Virgin Islands on St. Martin. This sample was taken on Pic Paradis, a 400m mountain on the French side. The Figure 2 sample was recorded recently in Borneo. Again, the consistent horizontal lines running across the

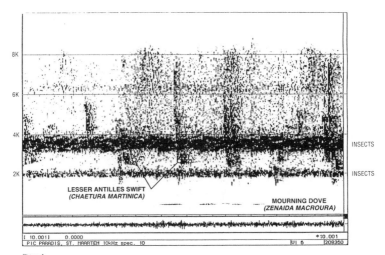

Figure 1

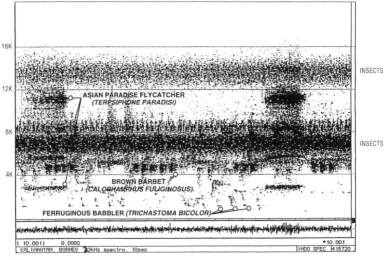

Figure 2

middle of the page represent insect voices. Notice the Asian paradise flycatcher (*Terpsiphone paradisi*) vocalizations at both the left and right sides of the page. Its voice is made up of three harmonic components called formants, and they fit uniquely and exactly into several niches where there is little or no vocal energy represented by the light or white spaces. It turns out that in every unaltered habitat we have recorded, many birds, mammals, and amphibians find and learn to vocalize in acoustical niches unimpeded by the voices of less mobile creatures such as near-ranging insects.

When examined from this perspective, territory now becomes defined in dimensions well beyond the 3-D topographical chartings on a traditional map. Furthermore, examining habitats from an aural perspective may allow us to actually date them in time. For instance, in younger environments, birds and mammals seem to occupy only one niche at a given moment. However, in older environments, some tropical rainforest animal vocalizations, like the Asian paradise flycatcher in Figure 2, are so highly specialized that their voices occupy several niches of the audio bio-spectrum at the same time, thus laying territorial claim to several channels at once—a trait that must have taken a particularly long time to develop.

These types of observations may be able to reveal a great deal more about the ways in which birds respond to the sounds of their environment. For example, many migrating eastern American warblers, able to learn only one song and call in their lifetime, find themselves unable to adjust to the changes in ambient sound when they fly to their disappearing Caribbean and Latin American winter nesting grounds. Where these environments have been deforested, and when birds try to move to nearby and ostensibly similar or secondary growth habitats, they sometimes discover that they are unable to be heard. Our recordings are beginning to show a strong likelihood that survival might be impaired because territorial and/or gender-related communications are masked.

To obtain these recordings, we typically spend 500 hours on site to get fifteen minutes of usable material—a ratio of 2,000-to-1. The long wait is due primarily to human-induced mechanical noise such as chain saws (heard from twenty miles away), aircraft, and motorized riverboats. Mechanical noise is endemic and nearly universal. It has become so virulent that we are now beginning to include it as a component of niche studies to see how it affects creature voices.

After my experience in Kenya, the recording of ambient sound as a field endeavor became more prevalent. Partially out of boredom while waiting for creature events to occur, we recorded pure ambient sounds to give ourselves something to do. However, little by little, I began to realize that what is represented is indeed an *animal orchestra* with each creature vocalizing in its own niche. I noticed that when a bird sang or a mammal or amphibian vocalized, the voices appeared to fit in relation to all of the natural sounds of the immediate environment in terms of frequency and the rhythm patterns in which sound is delivered. Over a number of years, I would return to the same sites only to find, when the recordings were analyzed, that each place showed incredible bio-acoustic continuity—much like we would expect to find from fingerprint matching. The bird, mammal, and frog vocalizations we recorded all seemed to fit neatly into their respective niches. And the unique sound groupings from each of these locations all remained the same (given time of year, day, and weather patterns) no matter where we worked. I refer to this combination of creature voices as a *biophony,* the combined sound that whole groups of living organisms produce in any given biome. Furthermore, the sounds of each of these zones are so singular and important to creature life in a given location that if one creature stops vocalizing, another immediately joins the chorus to keep the acoustical integrity of the habitats intact.

If, as I am suggesting, the ambient sound of primary growth habitats functions much as a modern-day orchestra with each creature voice occupying its own place on the environmental musical staff relative to frequency, amplitude, timbre, and duration of sound, then there may also be a clear acoustical message being sent as to the biological integrity of these sites.

It appears that ancient human beings learned well the lessons imparted by natural sounds. Their lives depended as much (if not more) on their ability to hear and understand the biophonies of their surroundings as on visual cues. Small enclaves of indigenous people—such as the Jivaro and other tribes of the Amazon Basin, and the Bayaka of the Central African Republic—survive using this information today. Not only can these extraordinary forest-dwellers distinguish one creature sound from another within a din of noise, but they can recognize the subtle differences in sound between various mini-habitats as small as twenty square meters in a forest, even when these areas appear to have visually identical biological and geological components. Even when traveling in total darkness, these people seem able to determine their exact location simply by listening. Moreover, after closely observing chimpanzees, mountain gorillas, and orang-utans pounding out complex rhythms on the buttresses of rainforest trees, I cannot help but be struck by the articulation of their message, its effect on other primates within hearing range, and the natural origins of the human art of drumming and making music—particularly when combined with the rest of the forest sounds.

Experienced music composers know that in order to achieve an unimpeded resonance, the sound of each instrument must have its own unique voice and place in the spectrum of events being orchestrated. Too little attention has been paid to the possibility that insects, birds, and mammals in any given environment have been finding their aural niche since the beginning of time—and much more successfully then we might have imagined. Indeed, a graphic printout of the diversity and structure of natural sounds from a rainforest graphically demonstrates very special relationships of many insects, birds, mammals, and amphibians to each other. A complex vital beauty emerges that the best of sonic artists in Western culture have yet to achieve. It is my hunch that the early human development of sound arts owes a great deal to the "noise" of our natural environments.

I believe that this newly discovered evidence points to the roots of ancient musical composition. One only needs to hear the compelling music of the Bayaka (*Bayaka: The Extraordinary Music of the Babenzélé Pygmies,* by Louis Sarno, Ellipsis Arts, 1996, a book and compact disc), to hear the connection. Described by Sarno as "one of the hidden glories of humanity," Bayaka music is recognized by its emphasis on full, rich voices and bright-sounding harmonies. The sonorous textures, polyrhythms, and dissonance all seem to flow from and be influenced by the natural sounds from the forest which enfolds them—a feature that both Sarno and I think is central to the creation of most aspects of their music.

Research continues on the issues suggested by this hypothesis. The study of acoustic ecology began in the late seventies with R. Murray Schafer and Barry Truax and is currently considered a valuable tool for defining the health of both marine and terrestrial habitats around the world. Adding this information to the body of knowledge is important for many reasons, not the least of which is the rediscovery of a direct cultural link to our natural surroundings before they all disappear. For the past several centuries, Western academics, writers, and artists have labored at some length to keep themselves and their work separated from the wild natural. This is especially articulated through the output of their craft. The use of the very word "nature" makes these habitats seem abstract, as if it has no particular connection to our lives. By learning to listen, unafraid and unthreatened to wildness and the incredible beauty it represents, we may yet be able to mitigate this collective deafness to the natural world.

Natural orchestrations—the sounds of unaltered temperate, tropical, arctic, desert, and marine habitats—are becoming exceedingly rare and difficult to find. The keys to our musical past and the origins of complex intra-species connection may be better understood from the acoustic output of these wonderful places, as the late Angus Wilson demonstrated in a remote part of the Oregon wilderness. Upon our return to the reservation, his mother, Elizabeth, told us a number of stories, which we recorded and edited down to a narrative poem recorded on our album, *All Good Men*. In part, it tells our story, too.

The way the medicine men went and got guiding spirit,
Contact with animals or whatever it is,
They kept on dancing every winter.
They got strong and power came to them. Power came to them.
Everything was different.
It must have been in those times when everything was different.
Clear air and wilderness, and they could get in touch with animals
*   like that.*
But I don't think they can now.
Everything gone—noise and all.
All right! Legend days will be over; humanity is coming soon.
No more legend days.
There will be no more.
And they will be sad like I am,
Brokenhearted over my last child,
Never to return again.
Death takes her.
And that's the way it's going to be.
I wander along only in the higher mountains,
And the heads of the streams all the way through.
I'm never down anywhere where it's civilized country.
I'm way up in the wilderness.
Years to come people will lose their only child,
And they'll have the feeling just like I have: sad.
And that's why these days we are that way.
Sadness comes to us.

As we lose the core of our own spiritual voice, we are beginning to learn that the isolated voice of a songbird cannot give us very much useful information. It is the acoustic fabric into which that song is woven that can enlighten us about our lives, our past, and the wild depths of ourselves that we long to know.

I had learned to expect nothing from my experiences in the wild, which is why they deliver such a sense of ecstasy to me. With everything else, I had so many expectations, so many childhood promises carried into adulthood. Security from hard work. Things to buy. Recognition. A place in the world. Most of these were fraught with conflict, remorse, and betrayal. This great stewpot, in spite of everything that had occurred, was a place where events were beginning to converge in a way that was to become very nurturing for me. Not, however, without a few bumps.

over the whole earth.

London

A couple of years after the release of *Gandharva* in 1971, Paul and I were asked by an American film producer living in London if we would score his science fiction movie. He also wanted to feature Gerry Mulligan as soloist for the score. When S. called us, we had already worked together with Mick Jagger on an earlier film called *Performance*. He was well aware of the level of work we would bring to this new project. During our first conversation, he mentioned that the film needed only fifteen minutes of music scoring. The production company would pick up all of our expenses but could only pay us $5,000—about a tenth of the going rate at the time. We would have the London Symphony Orchestra to work with, as well as the Bach Chorus of fifty singers. Although I thought the pay was low, I told him we'd do the job for the experience, provided that the music would not exceed fifteen minutes in length. I then requested that he specify the terms of the offer in a telegram.

When we got to London in late May, Paul and I immediately went to a film screening to determine which scenes needed to be scored and what musical mood each sequence would require. After several run-throughs, it became apparent that the film required nearly forty-five minutes of music, not fifteen. I arranged a meeting with S. to discuss the issues. "Three times the time, three times the money," I insisted. "And that's still very low pay for a full score." S., looking through hooded eyes, leaned toward me and hissed, "I don't like to be challenged, but I'll think about it." Paul and I, having heard this act before, were utterly amused and unshaken.

For five weeks, S. thought about it and stonewalled us. Nearly every day, I reminded him that we needed a revised contract. Meanwhile, we wrote our score and arranged for Mulligan to fly to London so we could record the new music. We found out later that Mulligan was paid more for playing than we got for writing and playing on the entire score! We had obviously taken the job for very little money because it gave us the opportunity to work with a full-sized symphony orchestra and chorus—something we had wanted to do for some time.

About a week before we were to record on the soundstage in Wembley, we hired the orchestra and chorus and arranged for the studio, knowing that in England, one pays for these elements well in advance. It was clear to us that the producers had already committed nearly $17,000 in cash for the orchestra and studio. The day before the sessions, we still didn't have a contract, so I called S., insisting that he get us the money. At one point in the conversation, he threatened, "You'll show up tomorrow with that score at the price we set earlier, or both of you are going to end up in the Thames with cement shoes. Furthermore, you'll never work again in Hollywood!"

After picking myself off the floor from hysterical laughter and checking the map to make sure where we were at the moment, I answered, "S., I want you to know that I've been recording this call all along. When we finish this conversation, I am sending the tape directly to our barrister so if anything does happen, someone will immediately know where to look. As for the session, we are bringing a portable telephone with us and hiring a security guard who will be in charge of the scores and awaiting our instructions in a car somewhere nearby. We want a check in the amount of $15,000 U.S. currency on the podium when we get up to conduct that orchestra tomorrow morning. Otherwise we will call the guard on the phone and order the scores burned." The next morning, the check was on the conductor's podium, and we finished scoring what in England was called *The Final Programme,* and in the United States was called *The Last Days of Man on Earth.*

At the end of the job, I felt exhausted because it was an ordeal instead of pleasurable work. While I had welcomed professional confrontations before and still had the youthful will to fight, this time I felt drained rather than energized, depressed rather than mentally invigorated. For the first time, I had a fleeting image of wishing I were somewhere else, doing something different.

Los Angeles/San Francisco

We came back to the States just in time for the release of our new album, *All Good Men,* the last music Paul and I were to complete together. We had other projects planned and had even written the text to the *Revised Nonesuch Guide,* which anticipated by several years how emerging digital technologies were going to affect music and music production in the future. For a year and a half, we had tried to interest Nonesuch Records in the project. In December 1974, they finally agreed.

The first week in January, we worked on the text of the *Guide* and sketched out the music format for the new album. Paul looked tired but nonetheless seemed excited about the process of updating our first album. When we finished the first draft, I returned to San Francisco to do some commercial sessions and to review what we had done. A week later, Paul called; after some discussion about changes that needed to be made in the text of our album, he said, using a newly-acquired Scientological expression, "I'm leaving my body."

"What the hell are you talking about, Paul?"

"I've decided to leave my body—dying. My set of keys to the studio and a complete inventory of our stuff are in the top drawer of my desk. Make sure that the pipe organ parts in the basement go to someone who could use them."

I had heard Paul say strange things before, sometimes to be shocking or funny. But this resonated with me in a different way. I was in San Francisco when I got the call from our Southern California manager and close friend, Bob Eisenstein. At the end of a concert in Los Angeles, Paul had collapsed on the stage, stricken by a cerebral aneurysm. Paul and I had joked about our respective demises, and this was one of the scenarios he had offered for himself, but I was completely stunned. "Well," I thought, "at least he went at the tail end of a standing ovation."

Paul was taken off life support twenty-four hours after his collapse. He left no will. (Originally, he had asked me to witness his will, which designated all of his earthly goods to Scientology. When I discovered this, I refused to sign as witness to the document. No one else signed, either. From the moment Paul introduced me to the organization, I felt uncomfortable about the defensive and obsessive nature of the business and was not going to see royalty proceeds partly derived from my work going to that group.) It didn't take too long for several of his family members, most of whom had been only remotely in touch with him during his life in Hollywood, to determine that they were entitled to all his possessions. The Mercedes went first. Then a lot of the equipment. I have no idea what happened to our master tapes because they disappeared. And finally, the Moog was sold along with all the rest of his things. By the time I pulled myself together to check out our office, it had been cleaned out and locked up; I had no recourse because, technically, except for the master tapes, I had no claim to any property. The *Nonesuch* project died with Paul.

I was, however, left with very fond memories of a good friend, the most charitable partner I have known. Until his death, I had no idea how much of an enigma he was and how little I actually knew about him. Although he often seemed dispassionate, his deeds affected the lives of others in the most generous of ways. At the hospital while he was on life support, people whom I had never met gathered in the hall outside his room. It turns out that Paul had loaned money, supported, or given shelter to just about anyone who asked.

When I called Denise to tell her of the tragedy and my incredible sadness, all she offered was an indifferent, "Too bad." She had always been jealous of my relationship with Paul because it pulled so much of my energy away from her. Oddly enough, it was just that relationship which had kept our difficult marriage together. It was to Paul that I turned for emotional and creative support because I wasn't able to get this from my wife. While she seemed unable to be supportive, my dependence on Paul for those exchanges still must have made her upset. After Paul's death, I knew with certainty that our marriage was not going to survive much longer.

I returned to the San Francisco airport the next day with the echo of my wife's words still ringing in my head, and I simply could not make the move to go home. Instead, I looked at the flight board, went to the counter, and booked the next flight going anywhere. It turned out to be New York. For nearly ten days I lay in bed in some midtown hotel, reflecting sadly on my life, my marriage, and my recent partnership. I felt sad that I couldn't trust my wife with my inner feelings or thoughts, and I was too vulnerable and raw-nerved to tolerate another disparaging remark. With Paul gone, what had kept our marriage together by default for all those years was no longer in place. I came home determined to resolve that issue once and for all. A year later, my wife and I agreed to divorce.

So they show their relations to me

The following five years were filled with a great deal of anxiety. I had always felt like half a person as far as our work was concerned. I think Paul felt that way, too. We each brought valued elements to the partnership and were dependent upon one another in helpful ways. Paul was fluent in the technology but not particularly comfortable expressing himself creatively. I brought the creative and conceptual ideas to our work but was terrified by electronics. And so we thrived within this delicate balance until his death. After the realization hit me that I needed to fill in some gaps in order to feel whole as an artist, I began to flounder since, having reached my mid-thirties, I had no idea what to do or how to go about it.

In a knee-jerk reaction, the first thing I did was to reach out to the community to find new talent to connect with. This led me to Andy Narell, a terrifically talented young man who had just graduated from UC Berkeley School of Music and who played keyboards and steel drums. I had heard him on the street outside my office at Fisherman's Wharf. We created music for a few commercials together before I asked him to help me put together an album I was originally going to do with Paul. *Citadels of Mystery* (Takoma Records, 1975) was written and produced in a climate of grief and confusion. I wrote it in the one small bedroom of the tiny apartment I still shared with my wife—all that I could afford at the moment. All of the usual aesthetic exchange I had shared with Paul was now absent, and I was faced with trying to connect creatively with virtual strangers. No one had any idea what I would be able to do alone, least of all me.

Takoma Records, a subsidiary of Chrysalis, bought the project. We put together a very sympathetic and wonderful team of musicians, including Andy Narell, Mark Isham, Chris Michie, George Marsh, Ray Rivamonte, Mel Martin, Kenneth Nash, Glenn Cronkhite, and Dave Dunaway, and the album was recorded in the fall. The theme of the album was cities and peoples mysteriously lost to the ravages of time, greed, and nature. Of the forty-five albums I've recorded, it is probably the best music I have ever done. Composed at a time of great loss, I completely immersed myself in the process of creating music that described my feelings about life, work, and the future I would have to face without a close friend and partner. Every time I hear it, its lyricism makes me hopeful.

Unfortunately, Takoma Records was poorly run. The graphics for *Citadels* were badly designed and the title misprinted. Two of the three words were missing. "No problem," quipped the illiterate artists and repertoire manager at Takoma. "No one will notice." There was a lag time of two years before it was finally released. And there was no budget to promote it. Although this was not atypical, I was very disheartened by the handling of our work. Then, in a surprise move, Mobile Fidelity, a premium label, licensed and remastered the album, redesigned the cover, and sold many more copies than any of us expected. I never saw a dime of royalties from that arrangement because of the deal made with Takoma. Fantasy Records in Berkeley, California, now claims to own the master but has shown no interest in releasing it.

To pay my rent, I continued to create and produce music for commercials in San Francisco, Los Angeles, and New York, but the market was quickly becoming more competitive. I felt burned out and weary from the large amount of hype and little return. The next four years of my life were a blur. However, I did find the time to get into the field and record sounds from the wild. This re-energized me every time. Strangely, the more I did this, the more I was drawn away from traditional music. But the remote places where recordable animals still lived were mostly research stations that were difficult to get permission to work in as an artist. I had no idea how to make a living doing what I loved most.

———

In 1979, I was working as a synthesist on the score for *Apocalypse Now* with David Shire, the first of the film's many composers. It was my 133rd film contribution, and I felt certain that a more brilliant piece of film music had not been written. But Shire's wife, Thalia, Francis Coppola's sister, began to have an affair with someone back East. When he found out, the ever-nepotistic Francis fired David. As I had been working for David, I was fired also. Coppola's father, Carmine, a composer of modest film talent who was a flute player in Toscanini's NBC Symphony Orchestra in the forties and early fifties, was hired because Francis wanted something grand and operatic and felt that Carmine had the experience.

Being fired from Shire's group gave me the opportunity to apply to go to the Antarctic to work and record for that December and January. However, the National Science Foundation wouldn't approve my application. "There are only 1100 beds on the entire land mass and no room for artists," I was told. "If you're a scientist and are part of an ongoing project, we've got room."

Undaunted, I returned home, determined to scale down my commitments. I let my secretary and associate go, cut back the number of professional audio products we were marketing and selling, rented a smaller office space, and applied to graduate school to study bio-acoustics. Finally, I made up my mind that the outdoors, as far away from the Hollywood world as I could get, was where I wanted to be. But not, however, before I finished the ordeal of working with Francis Coppola.

After Shire was fired, Francis decided he wanted synthesizers to be used as the instrumental basis for the score. But he had hired his father, a man who knew practically nothing about synthesizers and not a great deal more about scoring film. Carmine could only write melodic tunes—hollow caricatures of Pucinni or Verdi melodies, his favorite operatic composers and virtually his only musical references. This was hardly the material demanded by Coppola's epic. Francis then began his grand search for the world's leading synthesizer players. First he went to Japan to talk with Kitaro. Kitaro, although famous and a name Francis immediately recognized, didn't speak sufficient English and wasn't impressed by Coppola's erratic schedules and demands (which increased my respect for Kitaro). After several months, I was asked to come in and take a look at the current cut of the film. I, in turn, hired Shirley Walker to play keyboard, then went into the studio to program the instrument.

The music Carmine had written was dreadful. We had to transform it radically to make his sketches work. Then we performed what we had rewritten and gave Francis some helicopter effects to use in the opening scene. Finished with our work, we waited for what seemed like weeks before we got word of Coppola's decision. Eventually, by this hellish selection method, he chose five synthesists to work on his film, including me. Over the course of the next six months, I was hired and fired six more times. In between firings, I went into the field, recorded, studied, discovered the nucleus of what would be my life's work, and worked on my dissertation.

and I accept them;

My doctoral work took three years to complete. Originally, my thesis was dedicated to the study of bio-acoustics. I began with a study of killer whale vocalizations, comparing the differences between captives in marine parks and their known pods of origin, and trying to determine whether and how the orca is able to alter its communication to accommodate for human-induced noises, like boats and machinery, in its environment.

The vocalizations of the animals in captivity sounded so lethargic when compared to their wild mates that I began to get dispirited. Also, as I became more involved in the subject, I was more interested in finding ways to express aspects of what I discovered in accessible audio art forms and not just through academic publications. Combining my interest in whales with my interest in music, I completed my dissertation and project in creative arts with an internship in bio-acoustics.

From the moment I completed my doctorate in December of 1981, I never looked back. I made the decision that the rest of my life would be spent working primarily in the field and on projects related to natural sounds. However, first I needed to find a way to make a living doing what I loved. I realized that I didn't want to get to the end of my life only to discover that the sole thing I had created was thirty seconds of music to sell a pair of pants. I had already been to the Antarctic to work on a killer whale recording project as an associate researcher, but, for the most part, had been unable to get an assignment or the financial support to spend extended periods of time doing more extensive sound recording.

The representations of the natural wild I was encountering in museum and zoo exhibits fell far short of capturing the essence of what I had experienced in the field. Graphic and taxidermy objects are lifeless; nature is dynamic and robust—constantly changing. Events in films and videos occurred in a time and space so compressed that the result looked more like images from a controlled zoo. Events in the natural world occur over much larger expanses of time and space— much too long for videos and the short attention span of the average museum visitor. And in exhibits of forest creatures living near ground level, the natural sound recordings were often projected from dismal mono speakers near the ceiling. The basic ambient sounds were so terrible to begin with that some exhibits even tried to lubricate the result with layers of New Age music.

Natural sound by itself, when recorded in the field, produced, and delivered well, might be only an abstraction, but what a lovely abstraction it can be. I could put a listener in a darkened room and play the vibrant sounds of a rainforest, conveying more of a sense of place, space, and dynamic than I had ever seen in an exhibit with false trees, turf, and lighting. And while graphic exhibits have always been accompanied by descriptive signage and text, sound was just tossed into the mix with no attempt to connect the visitor with it. Inspired by these observations, I began to dream of doing sound sculptures better than they had ever been done before.

Kenya

A year after I received my Ph.D., Kevin O'Farrell, a marvelous designer working at the California Academy of Sciences, asked me to go to Kenya to record specific animals and their habitats on behalf of the institution. His idea for an exhibit was to create a day-night cycle of sounds, about fifteen minutes in length, featuring creatures that vocalize at each time of day. Synchronous lighting (dark during the evening and night segments, bright during the daytime sequence) was to be used for the first time in an exhibit to highlight the drama of the daily events. I was given a menu of sounds to record, a small budget, and about three weeks in Kenya to get the material. Because of the exhibit's opening schedule, we had to record in February, the worst time of year to get an abundance of animals in the Southern hemisphere. As a result, we had to work very long hours to collect the material.

Just about the time I finished my degree, I married for the second time. Pam, whom I had met while writing and producing the music for a wine commercial that required an operatic soprano, was then an Adler Fellow with the San Francisco Opera. She was comfortable living outdoors, having grown up in rural Idaho, and joined me as a field assistant on this trip.

In Nairobi, our guide, Jim Simons, offered many transportation options, including hiring a plane, but I chose to remain on the ground so that we could record at a moment's notice if something looked interesting. As it turned out, everything was. The first giraffe I saw looked as if it were walking on a stage set. I couldn't get over the fact that this wasn't a large zoo—the animal was actually in its natural habitat. It saw us on the road but just kept on browsing. Everything around the giraffe seemed to fit. The particular golden color blending with grass and land, the sounds of other creatures, the incredible unbroken spaces, the special scent of the dry air of the high plains—all was wonderfully refreshing and new.

Because we were on a research visa, we were permitted to journey off the road and to work at night where others couldn't. This allowed us to avoid what the natives called "click-click" tours: Abercrombie and Kent Land Rovers filled with people shouting, "Look! There's a lion," then surrounding the animal just long enough to click off a few shots with their cameras before departing in a cloud of dust. Lucky as we were, we were never able to get far enough away from the off-road vehicle engines, the light aircraft, and vehicles carrying exclamatory tourists whose voices carried great distances over the terrain. But the problem wasn't always the tourists.

One evening while we were recording a particularly dramatic type of tree frog, I heard the sound of two men speaking off in the distance. It was dusk, and I couldn't figure out where the voices were coming from because I couldn't see the speakers. Jim finally picked them out with his binoculars. They were two Masai heading across a ridge better than a mile ahead of us, and my microphones were picking them up. When I handed the earphones to our driver, he grinned, looked at me warily, then asked if we were with the CIA.

For the better part of ten days, we tracked a leopard, hoping to record one. Late one afternoon, we finally had one in sight, actually sitting in the middle of the road, just fifty yards in front of us. But when I turned on the recorder, all I could hear were the strains of "Stop in the Name of Love" by the Supremes from some small, distant village. At the same time, the animal began to vocalize. Since leopard duets with Motown weren't what we had in mind, we gave up and decided to rest. The animal soon ambled off into the shadows of the evening light, and we never saw (or heard) it again.

———

After my experience in Kenya, I returned to San Francisco and created a series of ten-second sample analyses of aural events from habitats at different times of the day and night. The sonagrams, sometimes called voice prints, confirmed visually that each vocal creature was finding its own place in the vocal spectrum and that they limited themselves to certain strict parameters. The sonograms graphically demonstrated individual placement of sounds for each creature, although a great deal more work needed to be done before my confidence would be high enough to share this idea with others.

The museum exhibit had to be completed, and I wanted to make the technology work in the best way possible. The finished mix turned out to be sixteen minutes in length with events moving from the dawn chorus, through mid-day, afternoon, evening, and night before cycling back to dawn. Changing in sync with the ambient sound, the dawn sequence opened with dark blue lighting, changing to a bright white for midday, getting gradually darker as the sounds moved toward late afternoon, and finally turning blue-red at the crepuscular moment in the program. This was one of the first times an exhibit was brought out into the visitor area so that the display became part of the visitor's environment. It turned out to be the Academy's most successful exhibit up to that time and for many years to follow. For me, it also provided a new line of work to pursue.

This time of transition was particularly difficult. On the one hand, I longed to be out in the field but had no way of making a living or getting outside support for the work. In the field of science, ambient recordings were not deemed relevant since the paradigm was to record single species. For most Western exhibit designers, at least, the wild natural world had been historically represented as heavily controlled environments. For instance, individual species are still separated out, caged, and then featured as examples of wildlife. Lack of environmental context, such as the creation of spaces for groupings of creatures from a similar environment, produces a representation that conveys, more than anything, an inaccurate portrayal of the natural world. Sound in zoos and museums is still driven by systems where the visitor pushes a button to hear a sound or see a video. Designers still install sound systems that constantly repeat the same program over and over.

Through sound alone, I discovered that we could celebrate the wonder of habitat mutability while at the same time demonstrating their strong continuity. I began to think about production techniques and technologies that could best express this seeming contradiction of natural reality. With a few notable exceptions, attempts to bring this wonderful, ambiguous aspect of the natural world into our public spaces had been met with incredible resistance. The market for natural sound recordings at the time was extremely limited, and I didn't have the money to create, package, and market albums featuring recorded sounds.

As music was all I knew with any confidence, I continued writing and producing a few radio and television commercials and, as an aside, acquired audio forensic skills. This mostly involved removing unwanted background noise from audio tapes recorded by law enforcement and analyzing voices and gunshots recorded during 911 calls or the commission of crimes. I never liked this work very much because I found it too adversarial. Testifying as an expert witness seemed like part of a game that had virtually nothing at all to do with justice, fairness, or truth. More than anything, it drew me further away from my real desire—recording in the field.

With over 2,000 pieces of such music to my embarrassment, I began winding down my commercial music business. I had my new degree proudly in hand and finally realized what I genuinely loved to do. Every time I was faced with writing another piece of commercial music or testifying on behalf of another drug dealer or murderer, the tension overwhelmed my ability to perform very well. I was beginning to see more and more that both fields were useless, wasteful, and consisted of fundamentally unethical work that only brought in a few bucks and nothing else of human value for me.

Almost everyone I knew in advertising appeared to be encouraging other people to buy inferior or unnecessary products they clearly didn't have any use for. I knew that many of the industries I was working for were doing damage to the natural and human environments. We were all participants in a dreadful waste of resources: intellectual, natural, and creative. I wanted no further part of the action. One international advertising agency, in particular, unwittingly provided the final impetus.

———

Late in 1984, I received a call from an executive producer of a large advertising agency with offices in San Francisco. The producer asked if I would create a demo with full orchestration and singers for a well-known, multi-million dollar communications account. The producer told me that I had to have the music "in the can" within twenty-four hours, and there was only $1,000 left in the budget. Moreover, he explained that two other music houses were also doing a version, and the commercial would be tested with focus groups for the best response. The winner, I was assured, would get to produce the national spot, which meant a fair amount of money. I agreed to do the music with the understanding that we would get the contract if our music won. However, the caller had a questionable reputation among suppliers; to make certain I didn't misread the offer, I secretly recorded our conversation.

After writing and producing the music, I delivered it to the agency and was told the results of the market testing would be available in a month. After seven weeks of waiting, I called the associate producer to find out where things stood. Not trusting her either, I decided to record that conversation, as well. After hedging for some time, she told us her boss had decided that even though our spot had won the market test, we were not getting the job. I called her boss immediately, continuing to record the conversation, only to be told that the job went to another music house because the executive and the winning music producer were friends. Furthermore, if we were smart, we were strongly advised to fade away and not make waves, particularly if we expected more work from the agency in the future. "Mostly," he said, "you folks have a reputation for playing it straight. I mean, I have a child in private school, and my Marin house needs a new redwood deck, and I do have friends in the music business who understand what that means if they expect to do business with me on these very large and important projects."

Trying to control my anger, while at the same time grasping for moral high ground, I told the producer that we had been guaranteed the job based on our music having won the test market study and we would pursue it by whatever means necessary. Moreover, I said that I was tired of being promised large jobs by his agency—particularly those that never materialized such as, "If you will only cover and accommodate us with one more small production because we've run out of money and need yet another favor. Guaranteed, the next one is yours."

Then the stonewalling began. No one does it like an advertising agency producer—except maybe, a film producer. Our calls were not returned. Our letters went unanswered. The final straw occurred when we obtained a copy of an unlicensed air check of the music we had created and copyrighted, but were not allowed to produce. As the producer admitted to us, our music had been arranged by the executive's friend. Since we had the music copyright, we had a license to sue. Having exhausted all other reasonable avenues of discussion, we filed suit against the agency, listing the client as an accomplice for copyright infringement and breach of contract. We also called the advertising trade publications and released transcripts of the tapes to them along with an invitation to review the recorded material. Several reporters actually came to our office. One, who had done investigative reporting for another publication, told us that this same agency had been sued for stiffing suppliers in a similar manner during the sixties and had a terrible reputation for continuing the practice on the West Coast.

The suit approached several hundred thousand dollars. When the agency's client was ordered to give a deposition, the agency quickly decided to settle out of court, and we got a fair amount of change in the settlement. The agency finally dropped the music altogether. I felt like Brer Rabbit in the briar patch, I was so happy. When details about the conflict were published in *Advertising Age* and other trade publications, I got calls from music producers all over the country congratulating me on my courage and wishing me luck. Some told me they wished they had the guts to do the same. In the meantime, I finally had enough money to buy some wonderful field recording equipment I needed and got the time to record and do a little fishing in Alaska as part of the bargain.

During the discussions I had on tape, I was told that I would never be allowed to work again in the agency world and that I was "blackballed." My response, also on tape, was that if I had to work in a world with creeps like the one I was dealing with, I welcomed the option. I never did work again in the San Francisco agency world. And I never again had a knot in my stomach from distasteful, thankless, and useless work.

Despite this personal victory, it was during this period that Pam and I decided to split, having grown far apart over the short time we were married.

They bring me tokens of myself...

Over the next year, I spent my time developing the audio forensic segment of my business while recording in the field between assignments. By this time, I had accumulated a fair amount of natural sound recordings and had begun to acquire the necessary equipment to analyze them. So there was a natural fit between the sounds from the natural environment and the forensic jobs I managed to get. The latter paid some of the bills so I wouldn't have to turn to the commercial music world for work. Meanwhile, some of my publications on natural sound theories were beginning to gain recognition. The glimmer of light at the end of the burrow was getting brighter.

In 1984, I talked with Dr. Ken Norris, Dean of Environmental Studies at the University of California at Santa Cruz, about the implications of recording spade-foot toads at Mono Lake. He suggested that I bring a hydrophone with me to hear if they made sound *underwater*—something that, to his knowledge, hadn't been documented previously. On a deep purple, glorious, cloudless day, high in the eastern Sierras, my new female companion and I lay out in the midday warmth on the north side of the lake, thinking about the recording logistics. With my equipment set up by the edge of a shallow vernal pool where the snow had just melted, I dropped the hydrophone about six inches below the surface and switched on the machine for a test. There were no airborne frog sounds just then, but my headphones revealed a chorus of sounds under the surface that was utterly astonishing. There were three distinct types of voices, although I couldn't imagine what could be creating the biophony.

I recorded for well over an hour, using up most of my tape supply, before the sun disappeared behind the mountain peaks and the creature sounds abruptly stopped. Quickly, before the temperature dropped, I scooped up samples of mud into a bucket and carefully rinsed away the ooze, leaving tiny critters on the sifting screen I had rigged. What was left were mosquito larvae, spade-foot toad tadpoles, and several waterboatmen (a tiny underwater wood-munching creature). I had never heard (nor read of) this type of mix of creature voices—particularly in this type of environment. The thought that this kind of biophony occurred in pools of still water as well as on dry land was truly exciting. This discovery was the second of my few original findings in the area of natural sound, and I was thrilled to be able to share the moment with my companion, knowing that she and I were among the first humans to hear these creature voices.

they evince them plainly in their possession.

In October 1985, Peigin Barrett, Director of the California Marine Mammal Center, called me to report that a humpback whale was stuck in San Francisco Bay. It needed to be removed somehow because the Bay was not saline enough to allow the whale to survive for very long. The Center helps stranded marine mammals recover from illnesses and gunshot wounds, then rehabilitates and re-releases them back into their natural environments. Under Barrett's indefatigable guidance and fundraising abilities, the Center has become one of the most important rescue organizations in the country, providing aid for thousands of stranded creatures over the past decade and a half.

Although the animal had been first sighted on October 10th, the Center waited until the 16th to call me—as if I would know what to do with a whale stuck in the Bay. I had some experience with marine bio-acoustics and, in particular, the recording of humpbacks in Hawaii. As far as I knew, no one was sure what sounds would make a humpback respond with either aversion or attraction. Other types of whales, like the California Gray, frequently found their collective way into the Bay and just as frequently found an easy way out. But not this time.

The animal had moved from the open Bay to fifty miles upstream, past the Sacramento Delta, and into a narrow slough where it seemed to be trapped. Its condition appeared to be deteriorating: its breathing was becoming more frequent and shallow, and its skin was showing signs of sloughing. In addition, the animal researchers had grave concerns that the low level of salinity in the water would cause a fatal swelling of the whale's brain.

The plight of the wayward whale quickly became a media circus. Many names had been suggested for the animal, but when someone in the print media suggested Humphrey, it somehow stuck. The following excerpts are from my diary chronicling three weeks on the scene:

Wednesday, October 16th

Peigin, speaking in breathless, non-stop sentences, tells me that yesterday the humpback got stranded on a sand bar off Decker Island until the tide rose enough for it to free itself. She says that David Bain, a young undergraduate researcher from San Francisco State University, had been playing some killer whale sounds to try to scare the animal downstream toward the ocean but got no results—probably because of the poor equipment and sounds he was using, or maybe because the animal was under too much stress.

"Can you pull together the equipment and sounds to do the job?" she asks. Not knowing exactly what equipment, sounds, or job she means, I tell her I don't know of any previous event where a whale has been in a similar position and survived, nor do I know of any method that might work. I do tell her that I am willing to pull together a team of biologists and to research literature that may shed light on the matter. She asks me to contact Debbie and Mark Ferrari, a husband-and-wife team and two well-known observers of humpbacks, who are upstream near where the whale is trapped. I haven't got a lot of time since I am working on a surveillance recording involved in the defense of an alleged drug dealer in the Virgin Islands. I'm a sucker, but I do it. Debbie Ferrari gives me the full report in a measured but energetic tone of voice. Debbie also tells me that they have absolutely no funds for the operation and very little cooperation from the National Marine Fisheries Service (NMFS) people who are determined to direct the operation from 400 miles away in Long Beach.

Trying to establish the terms of my involvement and anticipating no payment for my effort, I tell her that I'll get involved pro bono, but I must be given credit for what I am able or not able to accomplish. At first, she agrees, saying that it is a reasonable request. I tell her I can immediately organize technical personnel, an underwater speaker, and amplification equipment for the following day. I call the Navy Postgraduate School in Monterey and speak with Brian Wilson and Greg Pless, lab personnel who generously volunteer their time. They have the J-11, an underwater speaker that costs about $17,000, and can supply the amplifier as well. As soon as I get off the phone, it rings. Peigin is on the line. "The whole thing's off," she says. "Mark and Debbie didn't like your request for credit." In addition, she continues, Sheridan Stone, an employee from NMFS in Long Beach, is coming up with his boss, Jim Leckey, to assess the situation personally. Because the whale has been in the Bay and Delta for only one week, NMFS wants to leave the animal alone to see what it will do on its own. I have a gut feeling that the animal will die if something isn't done fairly quickly.

Thursday, October 17th

I pick up Dr. Dianna Reiss, a colleague, at her apartment in the city. Dianna has her Ph.D. in Marine Biology and has worked with toothed whales for several years. We have known of each other's work from marine mammal conferences, and I have consulted with her on her various dolphin communication projects at Marine World. Together, we drive to the Marine Mammal Center to pick up Peigin who, as usual, is not ready. While we wait, one of the volunteers shows me a list of "suggestions" for saving Humphrey that have come in by phone to the Center. They have been flooded by calls from "experts" and the press, tying up their only two phone lines. Some of the suggestions include dropping ice blocks into the water so he'll be more comfortable, dropping a massive curtain (similar to Christo's massive outdoor art hangings) behind the animal as he swims downstream so he can't go backward (no one figured how they were going to get him to move in the first place), dangling a piece of raw meat in front of the animal to lure him, and other cockeyed suggestions.

Dr. Ken Norris is the grand old Renaissance man of whale research. One of the people who discovered dolphin echolocation, he tells me over the phone that he has been suggesting Oikomi pipes since the beginning of the week, but NMFS hasn't been listening. He describes these devices as eight-foot long metal pipes, about two to three inches in diameter, with one end submerged in the water. When the exposed end is banged with a hammer by people holding the pipes in a boat, the noise transmitted into the water sometimes induces aversion behavior; the whale, like the dolphins being herded in Japan to be slaughtered for dog food by this method, may respond by swimming away from the noise. He asks me to try convincing NMFS and to keep him posted.

A boat and guide have been arranged for us at the Rio Vista Coast Guard Station. Mark, Debbie, Peigin, Dianna, and Larry Burr, a photographer from Time-Life, and I are all on the same craft. The *Sportfish* is Jack Findleton's pride. Approximately twenty-six feet long and set up to fish mostly for bass, it is captained by a short, stocky man whose opening line to me is something about being a Vietnam vet and head of the California Striped Bass Association. He speaks as though barking orders to some unseen platoon over the deep-throated roar of his wide-open inboard engine.

I ask Findleton to shut down the boat and drift, and shout to the others to shut up for a few minutes so I can take some sound readings of the river and channel environments. By doing this we hope to discover what keeps attracting Humphrey's attention, luring him further from the ocean. We are now about seventy miles upstream from the Golden Gate Bridge in water that contains only slight traces of salinity. The sloughs are narrow trenches not more than forty or fifty feet wide—about the length of the whale itself. This is no environment for a saltwater, ocean-going mammal.

We head up to Cache and Prospect sloughs and find Humphrey exhibiting what appears to be feeding behavior, although no one knows for sure since no humpback has been observed in these kinds of waters before. He is leaving "footprints," the result of fluke motion near the water's surface as he swims in elliptical paths. This creates distinct patterns that define the whale's location and level of activity. The water is forty feet deep at this point, and we decide to do some more sound tests. We get only the sounds of a hydrophone that is beginning to malfunction. I change the coupling to my recorder and things quiet down a bit. Better readings. Better recordings. It's getting late, so we return to Rio Vista and San Francisco to prepare for an evening meeting. Mark sits quietly by himself and appears to brood most of the trip. But he and Debbie have lightened up a bit. I guess they sense that we're all there to help and not to "scoop" one another. They have worked hard and, along with Peigin, are among the most talented and dedicated people working on this project. For the past several years, the Ferraris have tirelessly gathered data on humpback whales and deserve much more credit than NMFS, which is getting the lion's share of attention from the press.

That evening at Dianna's San Francisco apartment, Peigin tells us that the Mammal Center group has been working on the problem for a little over a week. We go around and around about the next day's meeting with NMFS at Rio Vista and are thoroughly frustrated, feeling that we, as scientists outside NMFS and academia, have little power and no voice. We fear that we will be there only to help facilitate the will of NMFS, who have already made known their fondness for "quick fixes" through the use of cracker shells and seal bombs (both are underwater explosives sometimes used to deter marine mammals or fish from exhibiting undesirable behavior). Their other alternative is to do nothing because they feel nothing can be done and any attempt would be too expensive. No one has a budget to pay for a large scale operation.

We all concur that both suggestions are too drastic and insensitive. I propose that we need some kind of moderator—a politician perhaps—someone with enough personal and political persuasion to guide the NMFS to a more moderate position. I have already called the television stations, but they have more important stories breaking. Earlier in the afternoon, I had called congresswoman Barbara Boxer, only to overhear her tell her assistant that she didn't want "blood on her hands." No help from anyone else we call, and we have one hell of a phone bill. I'm getting the clear impression that Boxer's cynical response will prevail, and I am worried. In spite of my failure to rally support, Peigin and Dianna see enlisting a politician who supports environmental issues and has the connections to make things happen as a brilliant solution. Keeping the pressure on ourselves, we call Channel Five again. Tired of hearing from us, a woman in the newsroom gives us State Senator John Garamendi's home number, warning us not to reveal where we got it.

As luck would have it, Garamendi is home. In an excited voice, he says, "I can't believe I'm getting this call now. I came home for dinner just this evening and told my wife, Patty, that I was so frustrated because I wanted to help the whale and didn't know where to turn first."

Dianna and I fill him in on the scenario, our voices hoarse and failing. He calls back at 10:00 P.M. with word that he will be at the

Coast Guard station in Rio Vista the following day with an entourage of state, federal, and local representatives. He has also arranged for helicopters, barges, tugs, small boats, and any kind of personnel support we need. Furthermore, he will enlist whatever other agencies we need to help us.

Friday, October 18th. Rio Vista

At the early morning meeting, the one thing that becomes clear is everyone's concentrated resolve to get the whale out alive. All except for the NMFS people, that is. Early on, it becomes apparent that NMFS wants to control the operation. NMFS representatives Sheridan Stone and Jim Leckey inform us that they have discussed the matter with their bosses at NOAA (National Oceanic and Atmospheric Association), and they want to wait longer before any action to remove the whale is undertaken. Their primary concern is the cost. (This is the middle of the Reagan administration, and cost is the operative term.) During a break, I overhear one of the NMFS representatives in the hall suggesting that when the animal dies, which should be soon, they'll get the California Conservation Corps to just cut the thing up and bury the parts!

After Dianna and I present a summary of the known science, it becomes apparent that no one has enough information to make informed decisions. Given the unique circumstances, we will be applying new techniques, gathering new science, and generally flying by the proverbial seats of our pants. Garamendi asks who wants to work with his group as director of the scientific scope of the operation. Everyone looks in my direction; since Dianna and I have just given a presentation, it appears as if we *know* something. I do not raise my hand because I haven't a clue what to do. I, in turn, look over to Dianna, who averts her gaze. We both look to the Ferraris, who shrink back. By default, I am designated scientific director of the operation and quickly turn to Dianna for partnership into the vast unknown.

When I speak with Dianna later in the day, I confess that I feel we've been trapped and given a task that no one in their right mind would or should take, given the fact that we have no information about this type of situation, and the press will be in our faces every moment of the way. It is clear why the Feds backed away from the center of attention. If we fail, it's no big deal and not their fault. As both Diana and I are independently funded, and meagerly so, I figure we haven't got a whole hell of a lot to lose.

The NMFS folks check with their absentee boss, Charlie Fullerton, and decide to let the whale ride out the weekend without our assistance. They won't be pushed into action. In the meantime, they tell us to begin to prepare for the pipe operation, just in case the animal shows serious signs of deterioration.

Saturday & Sunday, October 19th–20th

Dutra Construction in Rio Vista makes their helicopter available to me all weekend so I can be flown out to view Humphrey. On Sunday morning, we get a discouraging report that he is nowhere to be seen. Later, Humphrey is located in Shag Slough, a very narrow, shallow, freshwater channel, a couple of hundred yards long and maybe thirty yards wide, located between heavily fertilized fields.

At some point, the whale had swam past the rotten pilings below the water's surface at the Liberty Island Bridge. But now, try as the boaters might to herd him out using the noise generated by their outboard and inboard motors, Humphrey seems completely unwilling or unable to swim past the bridge again. I record from the bridge and from the banks of the slough, hoping to get some vocalizations from the whale. Others prepare for the pipe-herding operation, which will begin sometime the following week if all else fails.

We are all feeling stressed when a couple of tattooed, drunk, young punks across the bank begin pelting Humphrey with empty beer cans each time he surfaces to breathe. Enraged, I scream at them to stop, imagining how many shots it would take to obliterate the fools if I had a .357 Magnum. I'm getting too emotionally involved, a biologist colleague dispassionately informs me. I have to be physically restrained from responding to him how I feel. Finally, after several minutes of the beer can-throwing, the CHP comes and intercedes. The harassment has stopped—for a while. I spend a lot of time just watching the whale and the enormous crowds that have gathered since the media have picked up this story. I'm frustrated and gravely concerned for Humphrey and for those who are really trying to help. It takes me a long time and a lot of meditation to calm down.

Late Sunday I return alone to Rio Vista to meet with Dr. Norris and his research colleague from Santa Cruz, Dr. Ken Marten. We try to record the animal in the slough once again. Over several hours, we get occasional sounds we think are from the whale. I think I hear some faint "click trains" that may suggest some kind of echolocation. If this is true, it will be the first time echolocation has been detected from any Pacific humpback population. My interest is certainly piqued.

Monday, October 21st

I begin to analyze the recordings we did over the weekend to see if there is any evidence of echolocation. As far as I can tell, it doesn't exist, although several of us suspect it's there. The clicks I hear seem to be nonbiological (mechanically or electronically generated) and are probably from the downshifting of gears on the boats in the slough. However, I recall that leopard seals in the Antarctic and walruses off the coast of Alaska generate sounds that give the impression to our ears of being nonbiological, so my judgment is suspended on this one. I spend many hours in the lab analyzing and reanalyzing the recordings, but I can't be sure. Norris and Marten do the same in Santa Cruz and come up with the same uncertain results.

It doesn't help that I am constantly distracted by calls from the Coast Guard station, the press, and Garamendi's office. After about eight hours, I return to the forensic drug case I have to prepare for next week. The defense has given me an audio tape of what the prosecution says is of a drug transaction between the suspect and an undercover agent. I have recorded the suspect using the same equipment, in the same location, saying the same things that the Feds have on the original tape. Even though I'm dead exhausted from the Humphrey analysis and the disruptions, it doesn't take much to hear and see in the voice spectrograms (voice prints) that the suspect's voice is not the same as that on the original tape. I figure it will take a lot of time to prepare the evidence for the jury. I have no juice for a trial at this point, but I am hoping that I can catch the FBI Audio Lab making mistakes like they did during the last trial where we met head-on.

Wednesday, October 23rd

Over the last few days, the Ferraris, Dianna, Peigin, and I have been in constant contact with eight leading scientists. During our meeting, we review the options. These include seal bombs, strobe lights, a large sling (which the offerer somehow expects a forty-ton whale to simply leap into the middle of, so we can then hoist it onto a barge and carry it to open water), and, of course, Ken Norris's Oikomi plan. Norris's plan wins with one modification: the California Conservation Corps will drop a weighted curtain over the side of the bridge once Humphrey has passed the obstacle so that he cannot return to the slough.

Findleton, owner of the *Sportfish* and leader of the boat crews, is assigned to direct a flotilla according to a carefully orchestrated plan we have devised. It becomes the responsibility of Dutra Construction to provide the two dozen Oikomi metal pipes and the hammers with which to hit them. The impulse noise transmitted through the pipes into the water will create irritating pressure waves, hopefully causing the whale to swim in the opposite direction. Peigin assumes responsibility for providing 100 volunteers from the California Marine Mammal Center. It becomes more and more apparent how important the combination of compassion and good leadership can be in mustering cooperation between so many groups and people. I am beginning to wonder what it takes to get this kind of teamwork every day. What is it about this animal at this particular time that brings people together as they are now? Why is all this energy, money, and attention being spent on the suffering of a whale and not the suffering of people? Maybe we need a whale for president.

Thursday, October 24th

We gather at the marina in Rio Vista just after sunrise on a warm, hazy, fall day. Debbie Ferrari and I are on Findleton's boat along with half a dozen or so other people. Each of the eight other small boats carries three or four volunteers: one to hammer, one to secure the pipe, and a driver to keep intact the integrity of the crescent-shaped flotilla formation. All the boats are equipped with hand-held radios so Findleton can coordinate the operation. Dianna is onshore at the Liberty Island Bridge with my Nagra, recording the sounds of the pipes and, hopefully, vocal responses from Humphrey as he nears the structure.

We arrive around 10:30 A.M. and maneuver the boats slowly into position at the north end of Shag Slough. The whale is sighted by Mark Ferrari halfway between our position and the bridge. The order is given to put the boats in gear at just a bit faster than idle speed and then to begin striking the pipes.

Until that moment, the whale seemed lethargic. I noticed his behavior, and Debbie mentioned similar concerns. As soon as the noise is transmitted into the water, however, a different animal emerges. Immediately, Humphrey responds by moving away from the noise. As the flotilla slowly advances to the south, the animal moves just ahead of the boats, now spread entirely across the entire width of the slough. But when the whale finally reaches the bridge, he stops abruptly, rolls onto his side, exposes a pectoral fin, and will go no farther.

It turns out that earlier in the week, when we went out to measure certain conditions at the bridge, Findleton's fish-scope revealed what looked like old pilings just below the surface of the water at what was otherwise the widest gap between the visible pilings and the deepest water. This space between the new pilings was the widest gap under the replacement bridge. Apparently the whale became aware of the old submarine pilings and "saw" them as formidable obstacles. He was reluctant to swim over them again, despite his swimming into the slough several days before. Perhaps he had hurt himself on entry and didn't want to repeat it.

Seeing the whale's aversion behavior at the bridge, Debbie shouts to Findleton to give the creature a rest to try to prevent it from getting stressed. It's amazing! Everyone is really giving their best on this project, and I feel in my gut that there will be some kind of miracle. There has to be, because everyone is behaving in extraordinary and helpful ways toward one another that, I suspect, they would never otherwise do in "real life." We try several more times in the afternoon, but the whale doesn't respond to our best efforts. Debbie asks us to call off the event. Everything stops.

Friday, October 25th

I forget that I have left my Nagra recorder with Dianna so she could do more test recordings at the site this morning. Bummed because I have to prepare certain material for the trial on that machine, I call a film sound effects friend for a favor, because I'm leaving early tomorrow and have lots of work to do before I go. Working on the trial recording, I am constantly interrupted by Humphrey-related calls. I try to balance the preparation work I desperately need to finish with what is happening at the slough. I can't help it, but I'm glued to AM radio and am completely distracted. The trial work goes poorly. The results are muddled and inconclusive, but I keep running the numbers and voice prints until I get it right. Meanwhile, I talk to Bill Dutra, president of Dutra Construction, who tells me that his crew has removed some of the obstacles at the widest gap under the bridge, but none of the submerged pilings have been removed since his crew couldn't secure the necessary hooks to the rotting timbers.

Throughout the day, I am updated on the operation; by mid-afternoon, I am not encouraged by what I hear. Then, at about 4:15, Jay Zeigler, Garamendi's press secretary, calls to tell me the whale is past the bridge. "Findleton and his crew have done it!" he shouts into the phone with a greatly relieved voice. "They're moving the whale downriver toward Rio Vista." My first response is absolute delight. Then I remember that this is a wild animal. Banging may have got him 200 yards past the bridge at Liberty Island, but the damn thing has about sixty-five miles to go before he's home free. That'll take a lot of pipes and boats—particularly when it gets into more open water several miles across from shore to shore.

Saturday, October 26th

I arrive early evening in St. Croix for the trial. When I check into my hotel, there is already a stack of messages from Rio Vista and the press—all of them urgent. When I call Garamendi's office, I learn that the whale had been brought back to the Rio Vista Bridge, and he wouldn't go under. In apparent frustration and without consulting the others involved, Stone sneaked a rifle or shotgun aboard Findleton's boat and fired a seal bomb somewhere behind the whale in front of a crowd of 10,000 people! Shortly afterwards, Humphrey beached himself. I have been gone only a few hours but feel completely betrayed by Stone and Leckey's behavior. I am very angry and, at the same time, feel powerless.

If only I can get hold of a copy of the Marine Mammal Protection Act, maybe, just maybe, there's something there that will help us. I ask Michael Joseph, the public defender, if I can use his law library. Alone in the stuffy room, I spend the entire evening reviewing the document. The text spells out clearly that Stone's action is illegal and punishable by heavy fines and a jail sentence. I want to see him and his boss arrested and am determined to send a message.

I call Garamendi around 10:00 P.M. PST (it is already 2:00 A.M. where I am). I read him the part of the Marine Mammal Act that applies to harassment and tell him what I want done. He tells me he felt the same way, but it is more important to consider what the results will be if we proceed with my scenario. After considerable discussion, I am convinced that if the whale has any chance, we will need all the government help we can get. Stone calls a while later, and we talk about many things. He cools off. I cool off. We are compelled to work on the same team—for the moment. I begin to get back to the task at hand. An innocent man is faced with a long jail term if I don't get my presentation straight for Monday's trial.

Until I return home on Tuesday evening, I keep constantly informed of the events back in Rio Vista, learning that Humphrey has moved upstream and downstream many miles in the Sacramento River. Findleton and his crew will move him five to ten miles toward the Bay but have to abandon the effort when it gets dark. No one knows what happens each night, but nearly every dawn, the whale is found again upriver closer to Rio Vista. By now everyone is frustrated, and NMFS has cut back their operation considerably. Money is the issue, they tell us. But we know that the issue is control. When I get home on October 29, I call Garamendi's office to find that one last effort is being mounted. We are all to meet at the California Water Resources Board in Sacramento for a national teleconference of scientists and relevant parties that Dianna and I have assembled.

Thursday, October 31st. Sacramento

Before the meeting, I call my office for messages and find that Michael Joseph's client has been acquitted on all charges. A poll of the jury afterwards concludes that my testimony was critical to their decision.

Since we were up against the FBI's elaborately fabricated testimony, the day begins well.

At the meeting, Lou Herman, via telephone from the University of Hawaii, suggests that it might be worthwhile to try a luring method. He says that his research group has performed some playback experiments in Hawaii—using humpback feeding sounds—that produced strong approach responses. He suggests that if we use a suitable audio production system, such as a J-11 underwater speaker, and locate it downstream of the animal, luring might be successful.

Herman tells us that he was surprised that the experiment worked so well, mostly because humpback whales are not known to feed in Hawaiian waters. Even so, he says the animals were more attracted to the feeding sounds than to any other humpback or synthetic sounds that were introduced in the experiment. He suggests that we use his sounds for short periods of time until the animal is attracted, then turn them off for a while, beginning again when the animal gets off track. He offers to send us a tape but patronizingly reminds us (as if we are idiots and don't understand the technologies) that we need to use proper playback equipment. We accept his offer, getting a backup source for the same types of Alaskan humpback feeding sounds from Duane Johnson of California Fish and Game in case Herman's recordings don't work.

By the end of the conference, we determine that the only method we know for certain that works is the Oikomi process. Despite his obvious reluctance, Fullerton offers us a chance to try the luring method.

Friday & Saturday, November 1st-2nd

A package arrives at my lab from Herman. It contains a standard audio cassette tape and a short letter. The letter tells me that the tape is a twenty minute loop, originally played back on a Sony cassette recorder and using an 800 watt amplifier with a J-11 underwater speaker. It also says that the animals were lured from as far away as two kilometers (a mile and a quarter). I know perfectly well that the J-11 can't handle 800 watts since it's rated at 200 and will blow if you give it that much power. I also know that sound travels faster and farther in water; two kilometers is nothing unusual. As for the decibel rating provided, I have no faith in Herman's data because he gave us no information about the power output or how, and under what conditions, his instrumentation was calibrated. Furthermore, his students gathered data from studies with free-ranging animals in normal saltwater conditions, not a trapped animal in a freshwater river and slough probably suffering from disorientation and considerable stress, not to mention edema. Finally, there is no information provided about the duration of the playback tests his students had done. Both Dianna and I are concerned that Humphrey will eventually habituate himself to the repeated sounds and discount them as irrelevant noise.

Field recordings made for experiments are typically of a poor quality. However, when I play Herman's cassette on my machine, the quality of the copy is really dreadful and confirms my worst fears. Aside from the whale vocalizations we need, it contains lots of extraneous noise. Furthermore, each segment of the loop is extremely short in duration. It contains basically one segment, fifty-five seconds in length, which is then repeated over and over. This may have worked in Hawaii under relaxed conditions, but I know our situation is much more problematic.

I call Dianna to see if she can find out who did the original recordings and experiments. I want to speak directly with Herman's students to obtain more precise information since I don't trust his information. Meanwhile, at my expense, I rent time at a local recording studio that has a digital Kurtzweil keyboard sampler and digital and analog signal-processing gear. With a digital filter originally developed for the FBI and the FAA to remove unwanted noise from surveillance and aircraft "black box" tapes, I remove some of the extraneous background engine noise on the Herman tape. This takes nearly six hours to accomplish, even though the recording is only fifty-five seconds long.

Then comes the difficult part. I know we will need longer segments, mainly for two reasons: the unique nature of the habitat and the habituation problem. I decide we will need at least a fifteen to twenty minute tape that, to the animal, will "sound" a little different each time it hears the recorded vocalizations. I know from my previous work that humpback vocalizations, while often similar, are almost never repeated exactly the same way twice.

After I've finally reduced the boat engine noise as best I can without destroying the integrity of the original whale feeding sounds, the short segment is programmed into the sampler. By subtle manipulation, I change the duration, the pitch, the reverberation, the amplitude over time, and even the timbre of the material, recombining and mixing various combinations. That way, it won't sound like we're repeating the same thing every minute or so. The work is tedious. I've worked on rock and roll sessions that have been easier.

The session, which begins on Friday, continues late into Saturday evening. During a short break, I call Dianna, and she tells me that she has spoken with Joe Mobley, one of Herman's students. It turns out that he conducted the Hawaiian playback studies earlier in the year. He also tells Dianna that when the experiment was originally proposed, Herman was not supportive, but Mobley did it despite his resistance. This was why, he explained, Herman was surprised with the results. Mobley also tells Dianna that Scott Baker, another student in Herman's program, recorded the original feeding sounds in Alaska during the summer of 1984.

Sunday, November 3rd

We meet at the marina opposite Brown's Island in Pittsburgh and wait for the boat Findleton has arranged to pick us up at 8:00 A.M. The

Bootlegger, a forty-foot cabin cruiser, finally meets us at around 10:00 A.M., and we begin to move upriver toward the bridge in Antioch where the whale was last sighted. Findleton and his persistent group of volunteer boaters have managed by sheer determination and incredible endurance to move the whale some fourteen miles to this point, but they have probably covered more like 150 miles if one takes into account all the retreats and advances they have had to withstand over these past ten days.

As we approach Antioch, we can't actually see the whale but hear on the radio that Humphrey has been sighted in the San Joaquin—upriver from where we are now, just around the bend from where we eventually want him to be in the Sacramento River. As we approach the Antioch Bridge, we see that the river is completely filled with boats, which stretch the mile width of the river from shore to shore. Helicopters from the major television networks dot the skies, generating an incredible noise because they won't stay at the required distances the FAA has mandated for this operation.

Charlie Fullerton gives a command over the radio: we have five minutes starting at 11:00 A.M. to try our sounds. If they work, fine. If not, get the hell off the water so the pipes can be attempted. I am tempted to get on the radio and tell Fullerton that whales don't operate on NMFS time and to lighten-the-hell-up. But with no time to think, we hastily set up our equipment. We lower the 120-pound underwater speaker into the water. A solid mass of stainless steel, a bit bigger than a large can of Crisco, with rubber diaphragms attached to each end, this device is suspended by two cables off the bow of the boat and comes to rest about ten feet below the surface. One cable is the electrical wire that powers and sends signal to it. The other holds the weight and secures the instrument. Although we can put a maximum of 200 watts through the speaker, we carefully set our levels at a maximum of 168 watts peak. The J-11 on this boat is the only one operational on the West Coast, and we don't want to blow anything. We are ready.

In an eager and officious tone, Fullerton orders us to start the tape. I switch on the recorder to play back the reconfigured tape and, at first, because I am below the deck in the cabin operating the recorder, I am unaware of what is happening. It doesn't take long to figure things out. Humphrey makes a beeline to our boat, covering the 400 yards in less than fifteen seconds. He comes so fast that when he arrives, his nose virtually nuzzles the underwater speaker at our bow, and his body, which by now is stretched along the starboard side of the *Bootlegger,* bumps the vessel—hard! The combination of the whale's weight and nuzzling motion causes the boat to list so that the port deck is nearly awash. For a brief moment, everyone is terrified that the boat will capsize. We are absolutely stunned and panicked. But the whale slowly backs off when I stop the tape, and the boat rights itself.

I yell to put the boat in gear dead slow. To our surprise, Humphrey follows the boat, his nose to our stern like he has just discovered a long lost friend. Perhaps he recognizes the voice. We move the boat a bit faster, somewhere around six knots, and the whale continues to follow.

Using the protocol Mobley described to Dianna, we use the sounds sparingly, turning the machine on when Humphrey seems distracted and veering off in another direction, turning it off when he is following closely in our wake. As we have over forty miles to go, we want to save the sounds so he will not get used to them.

The Coast Guard's *Point Hyer*, with Lt. John Carroll commanding, clears a mile-wide path for us on the river, ordering all other vessels out of the way. Mostly, the cutter is the only boat we see for the next several hours. It remains a half mile ahead of us. We are alone on the river with Humphrey and, thankfully, he never stops moving. The press helicopters are still annoying and, we think, distracting the whale; they are coming in lower and lower with each successive pass until, in one case, we see water virtually roiling in the downwash of the blades as one hovers directly above the animal trying to get a close-up shot. Humphrey's movements show signs of becoming a little irregular. I get the FAA on the radio and tell them to get the choppers and all other light aircraft out of the area. I ask Travis Air Traffic Control to divert all flight approaches, takeoffs, and landings to the north of the field, effectively clearing the area. Soon the sky is clear of aircraft and quiet again, and the animal's behavior is less erratic.

A bit more than an hour has passed, and we are making unimaginable progress. The animal has moved almost ten miles toward the Bay without a single problem, and we are all beginning to relax. Just then, Fullerton orders us over the radio to stop playing the sounds so he can arrange to have the whale tagged. NMFS had tried unsuccessfully to tag Humphrey when he was still located near the Rio Vista bridge. The tags always fell off, failing to stick to the skin. Dianna and I have no patience for this nonsense. Dianna screams into the handheld radio in no uncertain terms that if Fullerton persists she is finished with the operation. She tells him that there are several ways to visually identify whales developed by Dr. Peter Tyack and Ken Balcomb. We tell him that Humphrey, should he ever make it out of the Bay, is the most photographed whale in existence. Therefore, there is no need to jeopardize the whole momentum of the operation in order to gain such a minimal advantage.

Fullerton remains adamant. So do we. Since we have a powerful handheld transmitter, I simply hold down the "send" button so that no one can transmit or receive, and order Jim Cook to keep going. When I finally release the button, hoping to save what's left of our batteries, Fullerton, who has gone ballistic, explodes into the radio, warning us that he'll take us off the river and have us arrested if we ever pull that stunt again. Of course, we're not too alarmed; the issue, as far as we're concerned, is resolved. We have the sounds, and the whale, after all, is moving. Having absolutely nothing to lose, I countermand Fullerton and order our boat to continue.

One of the most remarkable things about the day's adventure is the way Humphrey leaves our wake for short periods of time to swim close to the shorelines of the small river towns we pass—as if he knows what he is doing. At Martinez, Port Costa, and Crockett, where townspeople line the shore, he swims over to the riverbanks and does either a full breach or a tail slap, sending great plumes of water up into the air to the delight of the crowds. We can hear the cheers a mile out on the river as the people applaud each display as if Jerry Rice had just scored a touchdown in the final moments of the Super Bowl. It appears that Humphrey is thanking them for their incredible support, and it seems like some sort of miracle where we have all, in an instant of time, met the Other on common turf. The experience is more satisfying than I could ever have hoped.

The other miracle is that this wild creature, which everyone thought was ill, incapacitated, or crazy, follows the recorded sounds for seven hours and covers nearly fifty miles from Antioch to Angel Island before we lose him in the dark.

The next morning, Humphrey is found off Point Richmond near the Brothers Islands, and the Findleton-*Bootlegger* team try to lure him again with pipes and feeding sounds, working all day until they finally have him past the Golden Gate Bridge at around 4:00 P.M. on Monday, October 4. Sick with a bad case of flu, I remain on shore in touch with the *Point Hyer* and Garamendi's office, leaving the final glorious moment to Dianna and the others.

⎯

Lou Herman called me soon after the rescue and tried to intimidate me by accusing me of all kinds of turpitude. When he got nowhere with me, he called every television and radio station in the area, bitterly complaining that he and his research organization at the University of Hawaii had been shortchanged, and his program, which had funded the research that had generated the recordings to begin with, had not been acknowledged. That didn't work either, but I got a call from Dianna Reiss. She told me that she was concerned about Herman. He was furious and borderline pathological about the lack of acknowledgment and had a reputation for being vindictive and aggressive. "Being from New York and a little paranoid, he thinks you stole his science," she told me, her voice shaking. Dianna feared that Herman would make trouble for her if the problem wasn't handled. She told me to call him, write him a letter, just do anything to get him off her back. She was afraid of retaliation because Herman sat on review committees for her grant proposals and papers. I called Herman, but he was almost incoherent with resentment. Since there was no way to reason with him, I terminated the call after a few minutes. I credit the people who do the work, not the senior professors who claim it.

Garamendi demonstrated extraordinary leadership qualities during the rescue. Peigin Barrett, Dianna Reiss, Debbie and Mark Ferrari, and Jack Findleton also worked heroically to save Humphrey. The volunteers of the California Marine Mammal Center, Dutra Construction, and the California Conservation Corps, all five hundred of those wonderful souls who gave their time onsite, are also true heroes. And finally, Mobley and Baker, who refused to let their so-called wiser academic elders dissuade them from searching out an idea, made an invaluable contribution to the rescue. For me, it was one of those gratifying yields that comes from taking the necessary risk with the natural world.

Humphrey was a hapless, imprisoned creature. It didn't take much projection to see myself in his skin. Many people I speak with feel like they're stranded in a slough or trapped down in a mine somewhere, hoping for deliverance and release sometime soon. The whale was lured out by dedication, hard work, and imagination, as well as an incredible outpouring of love and connection to the environment that we need to get to know again.

I do not know where they got these tokens,

About a year prior to the whale rescue, during the time that my short, second marriage was unraveling, I went alone into the studio one afternoon. Wanting to relax and think, I put on a copy of the Africa tape I had created in 1983 for the California Academy of Sciences. My Moog synthesizer was already installed on a table in the room because I had been using it for another project. While the tape of events around the waterhole played, I began to explore some musical ideas I thought might complement the sounds of topis, masked weaver birds, giant forest pigs, elephants, lions, Egyptian geese, and hyenas, and I hit upon some textures and musical themes that supported the original composition. I can't even remember at what point I turned on the recorder to capture what I had played. But the next day, when I returned to the studio, the basis for a new musical piece and format appeared on audio tape. I began to spend more and more time developing new ideas about sculpting natural sound in traditional symphonic form until I felt that the statement of themes and the fabric of the synthesized timbres balanced out against the textures of natural sound and supported the settings of the sculpture. I was concerned that with well-produced natural sound sculptures, traditional music forms would only detract from the beauty of the natural recordings.

Several weeks later, I completed what I then titled "Still Life at the Equator." The piece, about sixteen minutes in length, was submitted to nearly 200 different producers and record companies. A few were at least kind enough to send form rejection letters; most never responded. By the time Humphrey swam up the Sacramento River, I was ready to abandon the project and move on to the next distraction. While my days were filled with field recording and forensic work, I was constantly thinking about ways to release "Still Life."

The following June, several months after Humphrey's rescue, I applied for a job at The Nature Company in Berkeley as director of media product—a position not yet created. I felt that my background in electronic media and, in particular, in video and sound, combined with my credentials in natural science would certainly qualify me for some position, although I wasn't certain that I wanted regular employment. I wanted to meet with the owner of the company, Tom Wrubel, but was sidetracked, instead, to a lower-level associate for the initial meeting. I brought along a package of material with me as samples of the kinds of things I thought would be useful to consider, including a cassette tape of "Still Life." After the presentation, Wrubel's colleague said, "We are very busy now finishing our new catalog. It'll be done in about a month. Your stuff looks interesting, but we probably won't be able to get back to you right away. Leave it for our review and call us in a month."

Hope was dwindling. It was another of those many times when money was tight, and I was gravely concerned about covering the next rent check. Bills were mounting to the point where, once again, I had borrowed every cent I could, had no cash in the bank, was fully extended on my credit cards, had closed my small office, and generally had no great prospects of making a decent living. A couple of evenings later, however, the phone rang.

About 7:30 P.M. I received a call from a man who sounded like he was crying. "I'm parked by the side of Highway 1 with the top down in my Mercedes listening to your tape, and I can't believe how beautiful it is. I haven't been able to drive for the past half hour. Oh yes," he said, "I guess I should give you my name. I'm Tom Wrubel, and I was just driving up the coast from our store in Carmel, and there was this tape on the seat. I thought, 'Here's another one of those damned New Age things,' but it wasn't. Yours is amazing, and I am prepared to give you anything for it if you will let us put it out on our label. I've been thinking about just this kind of tape and didn't know how to put it together. When can we talk?"

I must have passed that way untold times ago

I met Wrubel the next day at his office in Berkeley. His enormous energy filled the room, and his eyes danced with excitement. I could see immediately that he possessed the rare combination of personal, aesthetic, and ethical business values that makes life worth trying just to get to those singular wonderful moments. He understood media and the messages it could convey. He knew music—rather, he had a clear idea of what he liked and didn't like. His late father, a musician, had written "Zip-A-Dee-Doo-Dah" for Disney and virtually retired on that note, thus providing the startup capital for Wrubel's company.

Although he knew next to nothing about the technical side of audio, Tom instinctively understood what worked dramatically and what didn't. In this he exhibited an unerring sense of judgment. His comments about "Still Life" ranged from problems he had with the title, which he changed simply to "Equator," to subtle elements in the piece itself. Then he asked me to fill out the album with a piece representing the marine environment that would work differently from "Equator." "'Equator' is a temporal piece," he said, being one of the few people able to make the distinction. "It begins at dawn and brings the listener back to the same point the next day. Make me a piece that moves through space rather than time. You can do it. Begin at some point, say up in the mountains at the headwaters of a stream, and take the listener on an audio journey down the stream, to the edge of the sea, and then," he thought for a few seconds, "how about *under* the surface so the listener can hear whales, dolphins, and even fish? You *do* have fish sounds, don't you?"

Because he didn't know the limitations of the technologies, there were no boundaries for Tom Wrubel. At these moments, his mind was possessed with the wonderful playfulness and creative thoughts of a young child, completely without ego. He'd call me just about anytime, offering a suggestion here, another there. He'd drop by unexpectedly to the studio and listen quietly—sometimes not saying a word—then leave. Eight hours later—at midnight—he would call to suggest subtle changes that, when incorporated, would ultimately improve the product noticeably. He was also a man whose body was ravaged with terminal cancer.

By mid-July of 1986, the album was finished, the cover was designed, and *Equator* went to press in compact disc and cassette formats. Wrubel aggressively promoted the product, giving it the outside back page spread in his fall catalog. Within two days of its release in September, the album had paid back a substantial advance and was in the black. Tom was understandably excited, and he commissioned a second album on the spot.

Other than my creative partnership with Paul, I had not found a connection as vital and exciting as my brief working friendship with Tom Wrubel. We debated and argued about many things having to do with product aesthetics and the nature sounds people would tolerate. The arguments were always respectful and supportive, never personal. Each of us understood the language, and we continually saw value in each other's perspectives, which went well beyond commercial considerations. Tom retained the right of veto, although he rarely exercised it on my product. I would carefully consider the points he advanced and tried to incorporate them into the sound sculptures before finally deciding whether or not they would work. Invariably, I would defer, because in most of the instances I can remember, he was right.

My second album was due to be finished and released by the beginning of 1987. Before I would sign a contract with Tom, I felt strongly that we had to establish a fund generated from the sale of my albums to help preseve the habitats we were recording. Prior to presenting my case to Wrubel, I made a ten-day trip to Washington, D.C., and visited—unannounced—the offices of many different environmental organizations. I was looking, in particular, for those whose resources were not spent on luxurious offices, fancy cars, and highly-paid officers. On one occasion, I was waiting outside the headquarters of the National Wildlife Federation offices. A stretch limousine pulled up to the front door of the headquarters, and John Denver got out to be greeted by the president of NWF. I just happened to be passing within earshot of the door when I heard the man say to Denver, who was then a spokesperson for the organization and a high-profile environmentalist, "You know, John, you shouldn't be coming to these offices in a stretch. It doesn't look right. Next time, for appearances at least, take a taxi." I turned around and went back to my hotel.

After visiting several organizations, I finally decided on donating a share of my royalties to The Nature Conservancy because, even though it had recently been having some organizational problems, the people there seemed dedicated, focused on habitat preservation, and provided a larger percentage of their donations to their stated mission than most of the others. With this information in hand, I went back to Tom with my thoughts on the subject. I presented to him the idea that not only would a percentage come from my royalties, but I wanted to encourage Tom to make a small contribution from the profits of the albums as well. "I am amazed," he said. "For several years now, The Nature Conservancy has been designated as a recipient in my will. But I'm not certain that this won't be perceived as some kind of political statement. I'm also concerned that this will be seen as some kind of gimmick. I need to think about it."

"But Tom," I argued, "the Conservancy is not a political organization. If anything they are rabidly nonpolitical and, frankly, that is quite refreshing for me. On top of that, if we can actually do something to help preserve these places by providing money and support from the profits of our endeavors, that is to the good, and it ain't no gimmick. I am convinced that, ultimately, everyone involved—your customers, your business, the Conservancy and their goals—will be well-served by this. At this moment there is no other partnership like it."

The details took nearly a year to work out, but, since 1988, The Nature Conservancy has received well in excess of $300,000 in donations directly related to the sale of my product.

and I negligently dropt them,

Following the completion of *Nature*, my second album with Tom, the Aperture Foundation in New York asked if I would be interested in going to Rwanda with Nick Nichols, the award-winning *National Geographic* photographer commissioned to do a book on the mountain gorillas around Dian Fossey's camp, Karisoke. Nick's idea was to arrange for a worldwide traveling photo exhibit that would convey the plight of the animals and their habitat, with sounds from the environment accompanying the show. With two albums doing well and with support from the Aperture group, I was eager to get into the field to work. It had been a full year since I had been in a rainforest, and I missed the energizing solitude of recording alone in the jungle. The Rwandan trip was even more remarkable because travel before the recent war was fairly easy, and the government was stable. Unfortunately, it would be impossible today to do what we did eleven years ago. Highlights from my journal tell a little of what it was like to record there.

Kinigi, Rwanda

It is a three-hour drive to park headquarters from Kigali, the capitol, and nearly twenty kilometers from the nearest town. I meet Nick at the small house arranged for him by the World Wildlife Fund. Jim, an American veterinarian from Seattle who works for WWF, has been hired to oversee the medical needs of the gorillas and lives nearby.

Somehow in this small, desperately poor country, Nick manages to secure a small four-wheel drive vehicle as well as good shelter, not to mention all kinds of other perks that will eventually come in handy. Late in the afternoon, we take a drive through the nearby countryside to photograph the Virunga Mountains along the Zaire border.

Sunday

Today we visit Group Nine—an extended family of about fifteen gorillas, and one of several in the area. From the road to the edge of the protected forest, we walk about four miles to get to the group, which is headed by a large silverback and comprises of several infants and mothers, as well as seven juveniles. As we approach, the distinct, spicy odor of the silverback permeates the air. There is very little ambient sound from birds and insects and no vocalizations from the gorillas, just the sound of the animals munching on wild celery and bamboo shoots. I am impressed by their size and by the grace and power with which they plow through the dense bamboo and foliage.

On this trip, the tourist numbers are light. Only one couple from Australia, Jim, Nick, myself, and two trackers. Aside from the munching, the only sounds I hear are the rustling of Gore-Tex jackets, the click-clicking of cameras, and the irritating mechanical whine of the Australians' VHS zoom lens. Luckily, I didn't shlep the cumbersome and heavy Nagra tape recorder on this journey; I took only my light cassette recorder instead. Today's a bust, having got nothing but human noises. Not a grunt from the gorillas. The animals actually move to within five feet of us, and, because of Mark Condiotti's brilliant habituation of these creatures to humans, they seem totally unconcerned and unaffected. I reach down and pick a tender bamboo shoot from the forest floor. It tastes fresh and good.

We are allowed to stay with the tourist gorilla group for only an hour before we must leave. On the way back to the jeep, we run into one of the frequent, violent thunderstorms that appear each afternoon during the rainy season. We hear a fantastic cloudburst, but I am too slow, as usual, getting my equipment set up because the components are so awkward. The recorder is large and quite heavy, the mics and wires get snagged, and the threaded mount for the tripod is stripped, making it nearly impossible to set the mics properly and quickly.

After the sun sets, we are able to locate a nearby kitchen serving dinners of *pommes frites* (the chicken, locally called *cou-cou*, has disappeared from the menu by the time we arrive). When we finish and everyone has gone, I sit alone outside our shelter to get a sense of the sounds of the place. It's definitely rural: I hear chickens, dogs, and even human voices from Ruhengeri, some twelve miles away. There are few birds, mostly because there aren't any trees left. The tropical hardwoods were cut in the first half of the century by the colonial French who occupied the country, depleting its valuable natural resources until their departure in the sixties.

Mark Condiotti, a young man from Santa Rosa, California, has been here since 1979, working as a biologist and habituating groups of mountain gorillas so that tourists can visit. He gives a lecture to a busload this evening. The remarkable thing that differentiates his gorilla work from Fossey's science groups, he tells his visitors, is the way he has discouraged interaction between humans and the animals he has laboriously habituated. While the animals are aware of human presence, they act out their ordinary routines as if we aren't present. "The gorillas won't crawl into your laps," he says to the rapt crowd, "and they won't grab at your equipment as the animals are often encouraged to do with the scientific groups in the John Lilly syndrome."

Tuesday

The sun rises very quickly at the equator—literally in a matter of seconds. The dawn chorus of birds, which may last an hour in temperate climates, hardly has a chance to establish itself, with only about fifteen minutes for birds to chirp, call, and present a viable song. Because of deforestation in the areas surrounding the gorilla reserve, bird sound is extremely light, undoubtedly affected by the stress evident in the relatively small biological islands that remain.

The Suzuki jeep needs some carburetor work because it's full of gunk from bad gas, dusty roads, and a total lack of maintenance. It nearly shut down altogether on the trip back from Ruhengeri last night. That sucker has been trampled to shit on these badly torn up roads. I get the carburetor cleaned out as best I can without the proper tools. At least now we can move about ten miles an hour, just about as fast as one would dare to travel in this part of the country.

A few weeks before we arrived, the film crew for *Gorillas in the Mist* had wrapped up their shoot; they left the already badly rutted roads in even worse condition because of the outrageously heavy vehicles Hollywood demanded to feed and house the crew. They also left a completely changed local economy in their wake. Everyone expects more from rich Americans, and when locals see us coming down the road, outstretched hands appear from everywhere. Also left behind were the stories. Poor Sigourney Weaver, we are told by one of the guides, she was really upset when her bottle of Evian froze one night in camp. Somehow she managed to survive.

After about two hours with the animals in as many days, I have not heard much in the way of ambience or vocalizations that I'd like to record. As I consider the options, Nick and I cook dinner in our shelter. The rain is beating so hard on the metal roof that it drowns out everything, especially the Elvis tape Nick has brought to play on his compact portable stereo. Over the loud din of the driving rain, I shout for him to save his batteries and shut the thing off.

Wednesday

Today we visit Group Eleven. On our way, we trek into Zaire over the border: two and a half hours out, one on site, and two and a half hours back. It wouldn't be so bad except for the weight of my equipment—about forty-five pounds—and the fact that I still haven't recovered completely from an operation in April to relieve my compressed spinal cord. I ache all over, and my left arm is becoming numb again. The Nagra is truly a pain in the ass. The mics keep tangling themselves everywhere in the underbrush. I have a hard time figuring out what to protect: me, from tripping in the secondary growth that continuously snags my feet, or the recorder.

Condiotti recorded a scream on his cassette, but when I hear it this evening, it is completely distorted. I am able to record nothing but munching, twigs breaking, and the constant rustling of Gore-Tex clothing. After we return to our shelter at park headquarters, we meet David Watts early in the evening. He's the researcher who took over after Fossey's death a couple of years ago. Very serious. Very shy. I suspect from the twinkle in his eye that he has a good sense of humor. From what I am hearing about Karisoke this evening, if I were there as long as he has been, I'd need *something* to hang onto to survive. I'll know for sure tomorrow when I finally get there.

Thursday

The drive to the Karisoke trailhead takes about an hour, though it is only about ten kilometers from where we have been staying in Kinigi. The altitude at the bottom of the trailhead is about 8,200 feet. One of our guides, a short man in bare feet, loads my 125-pound duffel bag on his head and begins to run up the final 2,000-foot, muddy, steep incline toward the camp! Within forty yards I'm exhausted, still not having completely adjusted to the altitude change from sea level. I realize only now that I should have waited longer before coming. But, I figure, these opportunities come when they come, and you either take advantage of them or you don't.

Along the deeply rutted and muddy trail, we pass patches of stinging nettles that penetrate three layers of our protective outer gear. We slog through mud that comes nearly to our knees, sucking our boots off our feet with each painful step. The climb is notable but nothing, I suspect, like what we'll be encountering later where there are no trails. I try to relax and focus on the moment, thinking well past my discomfort and shortness of breath. After a couple of rest stops, we enter a flat clearing that marks the place where Dian Fossey chose to set up her famous camp.

My first impression of Karisoke, being an inveterate Westerner, is that the campsite is rather primitive, even by Rwandan standards. Small tin-roofed huts are strategically placed very far apart from one another—seemingly to discourage interaction between the inhabitants in this very remote place. The cabin to which Nick and I are assigned is located at the far end of camp on the edge of the forest. It is made up of one room, about ten feet by fifteen, with two sway-backed beds and a long wooden board that is to serve as our kitchen. The floor is so badly rotted out that we have to move very carefully to avoid the trampoline effect of the remaining flooring or stepping through the numerous large gaps. The angles of the shelter are lopsided and out of plumb. Kerosene lamps, our only source of light if we don't want to use up precious batteries, burn oil when it is available. Small rats with bushy tails scurry over everything, never out of sight.

Fossey's cabin is the largest in camp and is located closest to ours, about 200 meters away. It hasn't been used, occupied, or even opened since she was murdered some twenty-two months ago. The place is covered in a blanket of leaves, moss, and spider webbing. It is late afternoon when we walk over to the site. Nick heads toward the graveyard just behind the building. He was last here in the early eighties, when Fossey was still alive. All the animals she knew and worked with, and which were poached or died of disease, are buried in well-marked plots.

I walk over to the cabin and peek into the bedroom where she was murdered. Even through the filthy translucent glass, I am able to make out dark bloodstains on the wall above the bed. I turn away, thinking of the contrast between the violence that occurred inside and the magic of the forest outside her window. We learn that Nick's return will be cause for the house to be reopened after being sealed for two years, but it won't happen today.

Nick caught a cold on the trip and has been trying to shake it before visiting the gorillas. We have been warned repeatedly about how sensitive these animals are to human viruses. Anyone with the slightest sign of a sniffle or other malady is forbidden to come anywhere near the animals.

I boil up some packaged chicken soup for Nick and get him to drink some. As we sit around a tree trunk outside our cabin at dusk, we watch a tree hyrax just above our heads checking us out. This Cheshire Cat-like creature, furry and brown, cousin to the elephant, sits in a crook between two large branches and looks very much like something out of *Alice in Wonderland*. Its wonderful and special screech-and-ratchet voice makes it seem much larger than it actually is. At first, I'm unprepared for the loudness of its voice and completely overload the input of the recorder I'm testing. Late in the evening, I finally have the right set-up and record evening forest sounds and the hyrax for hours before falling asleep with my earphones on.

Friday

We gather early in the morning to visit Group Five. It is about a two-and-a-half-hour walk through very dense foliage, replete with vines, thistles, and nettles that become entangled in everything I carry and wear. I have to learn to walk all over again—with the secondary forest floor growth, each step must be taken with knees chest-high. Because of the cumbersome mass of my equipment, I am always on the verge of losing my balance. At one point along the path, I don't see the mud patch through the vines and don't even know I have fallen until I feel the sharp pain in my left wrist. I get up and move on, but after about ten minutes, the swelling gets so bad that I can't move my wrist, carry the Nagra, or do much of anything at all. We finally get to the group and they are magnificent, but with my left hand useless, I am thoroughly depressed. I set up David Watts with the Sony cassette recorder and a pair of extra mics so at least he can get some stuff. One of the trackers walks me back to camp, helping to carry some of my equipment. So much for my first day in the field.

When I get back to camp, a guard explains that we've been moved into a new cabin. Our new habitat is much worse than the place where we spent the previous night. It's darker and smaller, and has less storage space and more rats. Why we were moved remains a mystery. A denser population of rats scampers across the food counter—not three feet from my bed—and then up the walls, onto the shelves, and across the ceiling. So many rats have accumulated in our cabin that their feet generate a noise like static on the radio.

I have spent the afternoon trying to address the Nagra weight and balance problem. Because of its weight, the mic cables, the mic mounts, and tripod, it is a cumbersome system to drag through the undergrowth. In addition, I have to take extra supplies of D-cell batteries (twelve in all) in case I run short on power. This adds to the weight. I'm constantly cutting the mic cables loose from stinging vines and nettles. These vines, by themselves, make even the otherwise unencumbered trackers extra wary of every step they take. The gorillas are always on the move, sometimes eating through half a mile of vegetation during any particular day. To keep pace, we obviously have to move quickly, too. Early in the morning, a mature female cautiously approached me while I was nursing my wrist. I tried to pay no obvious attention to the curious gorilla as she tenderly explored the canvas cover of the recorder and the cables of the mics. But no sounds yet. Tonight I will figure out a way to combine and lighten my equipment so that my hands are free. With everything we are encountering, I still feel a pure sense of exhilaration just being here and know that these problems will be worked out.

Saturday

Warned about the dangers of nearby cape buffalo that had been sighted early in the day, I set out on my own, exploring the many miles of foot and game trails in the territory. After many hours, it seems that the ambient sound across the river from camp is the best I've heard. I rig my mics so that they fit into brackets, which I secure with tape and thread to my San Francisco Giants baseball cap. That way I can get rid of the tripod and mic mounts. Once I begin recording, I just have to be careful not to turn my head too much so that the stereo perspective doesn't change too radically.

I set up my tent and equipment so that it is located in a clearing about twenty meters from where the forest begins, at an edge habitat not too far from a small swamp. Since early this morning, I have recorded bushbuck barks, tree hyrax, and many different kinds of frogs and insects. It feels great to get some usable daytime material on tape. By noon it begins to rain and hail with major thunder. I wait all afternoon in my tent for the storm to blow over. After dark, when the storm passes, I step outside and flash my light around the edge of the forest, only to see reflected back at me the retinas of many creatures, among which are some feral dogs I had been warned about and whose fleeting silhouettes I had momentarily glimpsed just before sunset.

Using a pair of mics that would withstand total humidity and direct hits from the storm, which suddenly appeared full-force again, I continue to record. About 2:30 A.M., the rain stops, and I manage to get some bushbuck alarm barks, bats, and a few hyrax before I doze off. I must have been dreaming because I awaken just before dawn with a start. I dreamed that something had reached underneath the tent and was dragging me out into the open. When I look outside the tent with my light, there is a large steaming pile of cape buffalo dung, not two feet from the entrance. I try to engage myself in conversation for no other reason than to remain awake long enough to capture the imminent dawn chorus. However, for all my careful planning, I am too far from the forest edge to get enough sound, and the trees are not of sufficient density to get the animal mix that I need today. At that moment, a quote by I. B. Singer comes to mind: "Man plans. God laughs." With another set of dead batteries and not much sound, I ain't laughing.

I pack off again into the forest, this time to follow the Beatsme group (some gorilla groups are recognized by the dominant male's name) with Lorna Anness, a young Scottish researcher who is working on her masters degree and spending the year at Karisoke. Trackers tell us that Beatsme is closer to camp, just over the border into Zaire, and the walk is not as arduous.

We stay watching and recording the Beatsme group for nearly two hours, recording nonstop. Problem is that the animals hardly vocalize while we're in their presence. The weather on that side of the mountain has turned sunny and warm, and the clothes we wear are dry for the first time. Lorna and I sit in a patch of nettles and watch as the giant silverback plays with newborns, juveniles, and an immature female.

We leave the gorillas just after they get up from their noon siesta. As we begin to pick up the trail again, I remark to Lorna, "I smell a silverback!" Seconds later, there is a terrifying, earsplitting scream and a lot of thrashing and chest-beating as the animal barrels through the undergrowth directly toward us. Apparently, Beatsme sighted the porters and got spooked. I just happen to catch a glimpse of him as his massive body comes roaring and tearing into plain view, displaying his canines. I had been taught never to run but to stand there at full height and take the charge. Most charges are bluffs, I have been assured. But when I see Beatsme coming, glimpse the porters disappearing down the trail, and see Lorna dive into a patch of nettles off to the side of the trail, I don't hesitate for a second before I do the same. I'm airborne just a fraction of a second before the gorilla would have made contact with my body. Suddenly the animal veers off to the other side of the trail and vanishes into the forest. All is very quiet for twenty minutes or so while we gather ourselves together, badly shaken but breathing, for the long walk home. My clothes are wet again. And it isn't because of the weather.

We return to camp at about 2:00 P.M. and see Nick crossing the river from the other side, returning from his adventures with Group Five. His face is ashen, and his clothes look like he's been buried underground for days. It seems that Pablo, one of the young males, had been provoked by someone and grabbed Nick by the shoulder, dragging him about twenty yards through the undergrowth, ripping his delicate and expensive 300-millimeter lens right out of its camera mount. Nick isn't hurt, but he is stiff and unnerved.

In the evening, we are invited to eat with the porters and trackers. They serve a meat and rice dish, which we eat without utensils in their shelter. Nick brings his stereo and plays "Fish Wrap," a tune I composed with some friends where the instrumental voices are made entirely of marine creatures that I recorded mostly during the course of graduate work. The voices were sampled into a computer, then played back on a piano-like keyboard. When he plays *Equator*, the first album I had done for The Nature Company, he tells me to explain to the men that this was the sound of a whale.

"A whale," I begin in French, "is a very large animal that lives in the ocean and breathes air. Sometimes it grows to thirty meters in length."

At this all the porters look at each other and break into uproarious laughter, some even pounding the table.

"Impossible!"

"No animal can grow that large."

"And what is the ocean?"

Rwanda is a land-locked country, and these men know everything there is to know about their forest. Only a few have ever been to a body of water as large as a lake. So there is no reference, no way to explain. I draw a picture. David details in ki-Swahili and French what I've explained. One of the men takes me outside and asks me to pace off thirty meters to make sure I know what I'm talking about. Lorna is laughing hysterically. They shake their heads politely but are unconvinced about this fool's whale story. Now that I think about the story from their perspective, I'm not too sure about the whale myth, myself.

Back at our cabin, I shake the rats out of my sleeping bag, where they have been eating away at the ticking. I give my down jacket a thorough shake as well. By flashlight, I try to help Nick repair his lens with the few tools I have. The damned thing has been literally ripped out of the screw mounts, and all of the screws are totally stripped with no way to re-tap the threads. When I hand it back to him, he averts his gaze, and his chin drops to his chest. He is not a happy man.

At some point during the night, Nick wakes up screaming, "Holy shit!"

"What's the matter, Nick?"

"A damned rat just ran across my face." Apparently, this ain't a great night for him, either.

Monday

We visit Group Five today. Things are getting easier as I learn to walk the special forest walk, and I have regained the use of my hand again. After two and a half hours of trekking through the usual mud, bamboo forest, and vines, we catch up to the animals. The trackers are simply sensational in their ability to find these creatures and lead us directly to them every day with ease. Today I am lucky. Immediately there are pig-grunt vocalizations as well as some gorilla screams, playing sounds among the juveniles, and even some singing! With mics snugly mounted on my head and not as many wires to entangle, I move freely among the group. I must look very strange to the animals, because they are very curious. Many gather around to feel the textures of the equipment, and some even try to sit on my lap. I ignore them, hard as it is with their obvious displays of affection. I completely agree with Condiotti's rule of indifference and no contact. No point conditioning wild animals to trust humans at any level. But the temptation is certainly strong.

I remain at camp to catalog tapes, catch up on my notes, make the mic mount more secure, and baffle the cables so they won't make so much noise rubbing against my rain gear. First, I break apart a pair of headphones and sew the headpiece into my Giants cap. Then I tape the mics in position across the top of the hat so that they meet nose to nose at a ninety-degree angle. Finally, I sew the wires to the cap so they won't rub against the fabric. This solution is still quite heavy and awkward, but at least it's more steady and reliable, and the animals have less obvious things to grab at. About a half mile from camp, I test my equipment, capturing delicate bird and insect ambience and bushbuck barks. The buck, startled when it emerges from the woods, comes across the trail to find me sitting squarely and quietly in the middle of its path. It pauses for a moment, takes a few steps toward me until it's almost within reach, then bolts off into the deep forest.

When we order food in camp, we have to write down exactly what supplies we need several days in advance. The porters then walk down the mountain—often as far as Ruhengeri, about a four-hour walk—to purchase what we want. Onions, potatoes, tomatoes, bananas, fruit, rice, and any other food needs to be stored in rat-proof Army ammo boxes made of heavy-gauge metal. The food soon gets covered with mildew, but at least it doesn't get eaten by the rats. This week, we've ordered too late and are completely out of stores for at least the next couple of days.

Lorna invites us over to her cabin for pancakes. She mixes up the batter in what looks like an old army helmet and cooks the pancakes directly on the metal top of the charcoal-burning stove, there being no pans to do the job. With jam she has made from forest fruits and sugar, we feast on what she has made. To save batteries, she rewinds the music cassettes she wants to play by inserting a pencil in one of the slots and twirling the cassette by hand until it is cued at the beginning of the tape. While she's doing this, I string up a guitar she has in the cabin and pluck out some of the few tunes I still remember. With Fossey no longer on site making life miserable for researchers and trackers, we can enjoy a few light moments at Karisoke without the reprisals she was so well known for.

Sometime later, I return to our cabin and chase the rats from where I want to sit. Having given up on my sleeping bag, they've begun to work on the mattress, which is now sagging precariously in the middle. I prop it up with what is left of my once-warm North Face down jacket that the company generously donated for the trip. It, too, has lost much of its down fill to the rats and is now pretty much just an outer shell.

Wednesday

Today is a very successful, if not harrowing, day. While following Group Five, we record a large number of different vocalizations. The animals are now so used to me that I am able to nest down with them during their afternoon siesta while waiting for the daily rains to stop. They're usually vocal at the end of this period, and my patience pays off immediately. Screams, grunt vocalizations, playing, singing, fighting, grooming, eating—all of the material I really need to create a sound sculpture—come rushing at me all at once in a ninety-minute period of time. I also notice that there seems to be many more vocalizations than what I recall Fossey noted in her papers and book, but I will have to check that later.

Around mid-afternoon, a large forest elephant emerges. The trackers are the first to see it, and they high-tail it for the tallest, closest tree while yelling, "*Tembo! Tembo!*" (elephant in Swahili). I am settled in a comfortable position, recording, and get the elephant alarm call at the same time it sees us. It is *very* loud. In the meantime, Group Five splits into the bush, Nick and Lorna follow the trackers up the same tree, but I'm left out in the open with my equipment, still unable to move with any agility because of the weight. Everyone is screaming at me to get out of the way. Reality prevails. I scoop up my gear and scramble up the tree trunk along with the others—with no time to spare. Now there are five of us in one tree, with me hanging from the lowest branch about fourteen feet above the ground. The elephant extends it's trunk in my direction, and it comes so close to my feet that I can literally feel and smell it's hot, rancid breath. We must have been up there for some time because my ass is numb from straddling the thin branch. Finally, after what must have been forty-five minutes or so, the animal lumbers off into the forest. After waiting for what seems like an eternity, I descend slowly, followed cautiously by Nick and Lorna. Elephants are known to return at the most inopportune times. The porters don't come down for another half hour. They must know something we don't.

Saturday

Today is a rest day. Nick and Lorna go out to photograph the four elephants that have been seen in the vicinity. I stay behind and play Lorna's funky, old guitar until noon, and then I catch up on my field notes and catalog tapes, and clean my equipment. Nick and Lorna return around three with no particular luck. About mid-afternoon, we are told that Fossey's cabin will be unlocked for the first time in nearly two years. We will be the first allowed to enter.

Fossey's cabin is dark with small windows; the light that filters through the dust and hygenia trees outside gives the place an eerie feeling. Apparently, when she was killed, her family came from Northern California to gather up her papers and other things they thought would be valuable, as her handwritten and unwitnessed will that left everything to the Digit Foundation was challenged by her parents and declared invalid by a California court. That meant everything went to her nearest living relatives, even though Fossey was reportedly estranged from them. Her parents ended up with the royalties from her book, *Gorillas in the Mist*, and money from the sale of the movie rights, as well. Allegedly, they were not terribly generous about spreading the proceeds where their daughter would have wanted them to go.

By the time we get there, Fossey's house is cleaned out as far as her papers are concerned. As we begin to look around, we notice a lot of intriguing books, including some rare first editions, along with other notable objects that the family missed when they swept through. One of the books, published in 1861 and called *Explorations and Adventures in Equatorial Africa* by Paul B. Du Chaillu, was signed to Dian by Richard Attenborough and was one of the first books published in English on the subject of gorillas.

In a dusty box of tapes, I find a how-to-stop-smoking self-help tape and a cassette of a 1983 Christmas party, which I listen to after getting my cassette recorder and some earphones from our cabin. The party recording is a raucous affair—probably lots of *pombe* (a fermented banana drink enhanced with a little saliva from the maker) and other beverages of note. Fossey's voice can be heard in the background, yelling and insulting some trackers or porters. I recognize the name of one of the victims. Because her French is barely literate, she is furiously hurling epithets in a kind of babbling Franglais at the poor, unfortunate soul. She sounds incoherent. In between breaths, which sound short, stressed, and emphysemic, she coughs her way through each diatribe. I listen for a while and then rewind the tape, not wanting to hear any more. I think about making a transcript or a copy but decide against it, even though this is near the end of our trip. I also think of erasing it but pass on that idea, too.

After putting it back, I wander through the house, looking for other things. On another shelf, I find a small vial containing a lock of hair. I had heard stories about a local witchcraft practice where a vial of hair is left at the home doorstep of someone you wish to place a curse on. When I show this to Nick, he gets really spooked. As his face drains of color, he tells me that he believes in the power of native rituals and prefers that I return the vial to where I found it. I don't share Nick's sense of cross-cultural powers of human hair and ritual objects, but I eventually put it back.

The kitchen is still stocked with canned goods and rusting utensils strewn all over the counter tops. The living room walls are papered with black and white photos of various gorillas, lovingly arranged by group. Although the cabin is anything but neat, everything in it has a certain practical, functional organization to it. I have no way to tell if this is Fossey's design or that of the investigators after her demise. The bedroom where she was murdered almost two years ago reveals more detail than my first observations from the outside: blood stains everywhere—on the mattress still askew on the bed, on the wall at the head of the bed, on the floor—and a nightstand with a huge hack mark deep in the leading edge of the top from one hell of a sharp and heavy object. There remains a feeling of single-minded drive and intent in this house, but not much in the way of warmth. Many artifacts remain, but they are arranged in odd places along the walls, counters, or tables.

Fossey's house is more remote than the others in the compound. This theme of isolation is carried out in the way the cabins are scattered across the Karisoke plateau site. The impression is one of seclusion beyond solitude, and there is a certain austerity in a place already very cut off and remote. Instead of grouping the researchers' cabin sites closer to her or to one another, Fossey preferred them spread far apart throughout the camp. No cabin is easily in sight of another, and one has to walk a hundred yards or more over muddy or treacherous paths to get to a neighbor's shack. This is hardly a site that promotes information sharing or a respite from isolation. It feels like a place that is specifically designed to preclude normal human contact. While I have enormous respect for those researchers who did and still do prevail for long periods of time in these kinds of conditions, at the same time I have a great deal of sympathy for those others not able to endure the separation and distance that Fossey's otherwise remarkable life engendered.

We are nearing the end of our month-long trip, and I dread going back. I've separated myself from the deadening opiate of Western television and newspapers, and my mind feels "clean" for the first time in a long while. My legs are strong now, and I manage the trails easily. I am beginning to recognize landmark references in the forest not only by sight but also by sound. It seems that every change of altitude and every few hundred meters of travel results in a different sound, as each microhabitat generates its own sonic fingerprint. Amazingly, I feel at very much at home here.

Myself moving forward

San Francisco

Before Tom Wrubel died in late 1989, he had commissioned nine albums from me. The last one he participated in was called *Gorilla*. When I returned from Rwanda with lots of wonderful material in hand, it was natural that we do an album with material gathered from this rare habitat. Before his illness almost totally incapacitated him, Tom dropped by to listen to the some of the raw material from Karisoke. He decided, even though he wasn't completely convinced about the project, that he was willing to take a chance.

During the production, Tom became hospitalized for what would be the final time. I sent him tapes for review every couple of days because I knew he still wanted to be involved. At three o'clock one morning, the phone rang. I knew it was Tom, but his voice was weak and hardly recognizable. "Right now, the album sounds great. But it needs more mountain gorilla sounds. More music. And for Christ's sake, get those people sounds out of there. We don't want people in nature!" He hung up before I could answer. As I was dozing off to sleep, the phone rang a second time. "Forget what I said about the people. Leave them in. But whatever you do, don't fuck it up!"

That was the last time I spoke with him. Tom Wrubel died a few days later. I felt like I had lost a great friend and a very helpful partner.

After Tom's death, I did one more album for The Nature Company. Called *Meridian*, it was based on a Native American legend of the "Good Red Road," a route often taken by Southwest natives while on their vision quests. For this sound sculpture, I recorded habitats in the high desert from Nogales along the 111 meridian, straight north to the Canadian border. With my colleague, Phil Aaberg, we set the sound sculptures to music, tracking spring as it moved north sixteen miles a day. The recordings and concepts were enchanting and evocative. A National Geographic team filmed us, including a scene recording ants (*Pogonomyrmex maricopa*).

At The Nature Company, there was no single person who truly understood the medium, and the accepted product aesthetics were changing within the organization virtually on a daily basis; there seemed to be a great deal of confusion as to what was acceptable. "Too heavy in the bass," said one buyer in her late forties, who had a year of piano in her childhood to her music credit. "Footsteps!? Do I hear *human* footsteps?" said another, echoing the late Tom Wrubel's earlier mandates. "Either take them out or turn them way down!" demanded another. "No humans in our product," she insisted with a certain amount of automatonic corporate authority. "Change the title," ordered the new president of the company. "Even though our customer base is educated, no one will know what *meridian* means."

The final product, while good, suffered from a mix of rather unfortunate corporate decisions coming from several different people, none of whom had the vaguest idea of sound recording as a creative medium, music, or their market base. As a result, the product fell short of everyone's vision. Phil and I were enraged and completely frustrated. Until then, I had always enjoyed the process of creating these special commissions, mostly because of Wrubel's involvement, trust, and support. He had the rare combination of creative intelligence and knowing what he was doing. However, because no one else at the

Nature Company expressed a clear view, aptitude, or language related to the work, the product had to be mediated rather than created as a labor of love.

By this time, I was working in the field some seven months a year and collecting wonderful material from Alaska, polar regions, Africa, the Northwest, the Rockies, equatorial rainforests, marine environments, and deserts. I desperately wanted to find an outlet for the comprehensive library of sound I was amassing. The Nature Company, in its chaotic state, was no longer much of an option for me, so in 1989, I started my own small record company, Wild Sanctuary, and began to release a series of different ambient titles under that name.

———

From the time of my early successes with The Nature Company, I began to do a number of community outreach programs in schools throughout the West. At first, these programs were presented in a straightforward manner, using the sounds of living organisms and playing them as examples throughout the program. But this type of presentation was boring to me and, undoubtedly, to the students who had to sit through it. Soon after our second album, I joined with a couple of musicians and produced a piece of music called "Fish Wrap," which was done entirely on spec. The tune was made up of animal sounds, each one coming from a marine environment. We used the sounds of fish, crustaceans, and several different kinds of whales, each of their voices represented a traditional instrument. The musical lines were created first by sampling, or recording each animal voice into a computer, then controlling the length and pitch of each sound with a piano-like keyboard, playing every line just like it was a traditional instrument.

After completing "Fish Wrap," I would only do kids' programs armed with a professional 200-watt studio loudspeaker system, a four-channel mixer, and my digital audio recorder (DAT) containing "Fish

Wrap." With the system cranked, I blasted the otherwise inattentive audience with fish music! First, this had the effect of being louder than they could talk, so they got quiet rather quickly. Second, the spitballs quit flying across the auditorium. Once the tune came to an end, I would casually tell them, "All of the sounds you just heard were made from the voices of animals," and then spend the next forty minutes demonstrating the point to a now-captive audience.

I would play each individual sound, telling the story behind the recordings and the problems I had getting them on tape. Then I'd introduce some comments about the dangers of working in the field. The stories described the rewards (other than financial) that outweighed any reasons not to do it. Then we'd talk about the environment, creatures, science, and sound. At the end of the program, there would always be several young students who would come up and ask how they could learn to do what I did.

Their range of responses was amazing to me. Typically, third or fourth graders would ask, "What can we do to help?" or "How can we do what you do?" The questions that threw me came from those eleven years and older. "How much money do you make?" many would ask. A young boy of about eleven or twelve once asked, "What is the most dangerous animal you've ever recorded?"

"Man," I responded without missing a beat.

"You mean, a man's more dangerous than a polar bear?"

"When was the last time you saw a polar bear with an AK47?"

"But my father says bears..." he continued to insist, and I knew I had lost the argument. Sadly, our deep-seated fears of the natural world are what we need most to overcome. But this response is, by far, in the minority. For years, we have offered these programs free of charge and continue to do so. As part of these school programs, I always try to shed new light and create a sense of wonder about taking the time to explore the natural world—things young students may not have thought of before. I try to inspire the seventh graders to ask the same questions as the third graders. I am particularly moved by the letters I get from students telling me how meaningful the program was and how it led to changes in their thinking, levels of interest about the natural world, and even the direction of their lives. I feel triumphant if one in a crowd of a hundred asks a meaningful question, writes a letter, or sends an e-mail to find out more about what we can do. These are the responses that keep me doing the programs.

then and now and forever,

As Nick Nichols was photographing the great apes of the world—
mountain gorillas, chimpanzees, and orang-utans—I began thinking
that, since their habitats are disappearing at a rate so swift that even
biologists are unable to grasp the full impact, we had better get some of
these places recorded and create a sonic record to compare the
differences between disturbed and undisturbed sites. While we have
some indication of the severe impact from the ways in which the
biophonies have been altered, I realized that a great deal of recording
work remained to be done. When comparing different biomes, the
sounds present in disturbed forests are less dense, or else they feature
animals that are forced to adapt to edge habitats (open spaces alongside
clear cutting) where the altered microclimate tends to be hotter,
windier, and more severe. This upsetting of the organic balances of
tropical forest life are as evident in Indonesia as anywhere on the
planet. My journal entries reflect some of what we experienced when
recording sounds there.

Indonesia. March, 1991

Ruth Happel and I have come to Sumatra and Borneo to record orang-utans and their habitats for a sound sculpture that was commissioned for the Cleveland Zoo's rainforest exhibit.

Ary, our guide, finds a small, local guest house that is full, but it has a very tiny room, open to the elements, with two camp cots. The temperature is in the mid-nineties and humid. Our host serves us a bowl of very hot noodle soup made mostly of red peppers. We are unable to tolerate more than a couple of spoonfuls even though we have had nothing to eat or drink since early morning. We are too tired to wash. Officially, the restaurant is closed, but no sooner do we try to sleep than activity on the road just outside erupts all over again. Sporadically, loud motorcycles arrive at the other side of our cloth barrier, the drivers asking for drinks or food. The innkeepers, friendly and accommodating people, reopen each time someone comes. When the procession finally stops and the overhead light is unscrewed, we are left with distant forest night sounds mixed with the coughing of both innkeepers. No one here doesn't smoke, it seems. We don't sleep that night.

Thursday, March 7th

Across the river, where the research camp is located, Ary has been trying to negotiate our accommodations since breakfast today. Turns out everything is full there, too, except for the abandoned "student quarters." The first thing we notice about the slabs that will serve as our beds is the box at the head of each. It's the place into which one puts one's head at night to avoid having rats run over one's face while one sleeps, we are told.

We settle in and arrange our equipment in a way that's easily accessible, keeping the things that need to stay dry away from obvious places where the roof leaks. After lunch we begin to scout sites where we might record—places far enough away from the river, the road, and other typical camp noises. As we walk, the first thing we notice are the small, inch-long ground leeches—tens of thousands of them—undulating and twisting their tiny bodies toward anything warmer than the forest floor. They eat through our socks and shoes. When we return to camp, exhausted from our day's hike to locate a quiet place to record, we find them engorged and attached painlessly to the surfaces of our feet and ankles. We remove our shoes carefully so as not to bust them open and spill blood all over the rest of our clothes.

The leeches are particularly attracted to the heat generated by the batteries powering my recorder. These fascinating creatures crawl all over and into the machinery as I sit and watch in amazement. On our way back to camp, we spot an orang and her baby resting in a tree and watch her for some time. She makes no sound. Neither does her baby. We also see long-tailed macaques, barbets, and several rhinoceros hornbills. It looks like a good place to be doing what we need to do. Setting up our equipment and picking leeches off our shoes, we wait for the dusk chorus, which soon reveals a wonderful composition of cicadas and frogs.

Monday, March 11th

For the past several days, we have consistently recorded a rich library of leaf monkeys, gibbons, squirrels, and a wide variety of birds. We just have to learn to stay away from the guides, who smoke and cough continuously.

Last night, Lisbet, a young, bright, and enthusiastic researcher from Holland, told us of her plight recording the clouded leopard. In three months of trailing the animal, she's never seen it, *thinks* she heard it once, and knows it's around only by the daily trails of paw prints, scat, and the occasional sightings mentioned by local guides. Apparently, she hopes to see it by chasing it down; I think it's a lost cause unless she's willing to reconsider her *modus operandi*. I ask her what she wants the animal to do. She tells me that she wants to see it just one time before her six-month research grant expires. With some thinly-disguised assurance, I tell her, if she wants, we'll see it tomorrow. She tells me I'm crazy. I tell her, maybe so, but I intend to see it tomorrow and she can meet me at dawn if she is prepared to sit for a whole day in one spot without moving.

Before sunrise, Lisbet meets me on the trail leading from camp, and we head out to a confluence of several forest paths where she has previously observed many paw prints and collected scat. Her body language and tone of voice betray a deep skepticism and little hope. I don't blame her. Creating what appears to be a ritual, I set up two tripod canvas stools and invite her to sit in one. I sit in the other, having set up my mics some distance down a trail that looks promising. The dawn chorus passes quickly, as it does in rainforest habitats located near the equator. We begin to feel a gradual warming as the sun moves higher. The dappled shadows of the light through the canopy combine with the bird and insect sounds playing differently with each passing hour. Four hours pass. Six. Eight. Lisbet is growing impatient but I implore her not to move.

Just before dusk, I hear a quick, faint rustling of leaves on the forest floor behind us. Turning my head very slowly to the left and looking over my shoulder, I see the clouded leopard emerging from the undergrowth. It is much smaller than I would have imagined, a little over four feet long from head to tail, but lithe and graceful. It glances at us, and I meet its gaze for a brief second before looking away, not wanting to provoke or frighten it. The cat moves slowly in a large circle about twenty feet away, and I notice, when I glance at Lisbet to see her reaction, that tears are streaming down her face. The animal continues to circle tentatively around us, directly in front of where we are sitting. When the leopard completes the first turn, I think it will head back into the forest. Instead, it continues to circle three more times, and with each slow orbit maintains the same twenty foot radius. Lisbet is now sobbing quietly, I guess hoping that she can get one last glimpse. After a moment or so, she rises, walks to where I'm still sitting, and gives me a big hug. I certainly won't ever confess the truth, but I'm as surprised as anyone at seeing the wee beastie.

———

The research station at Ketambe (Sumatra) consists of a few thousand acres of untouched forest that are nibbled away at by residents of nearby towns. Thus, the habitat of the orangs grows smaller with each passing hour. There's also a huge Indonesian black-market trade in baby orangs and other forest-dwelling animals. Current black-market rate: $100. I remember that even a well-respected director of a major midwestern American zoo called just before we left on our trip to see if I "could score a source for procuring baby proboscis monkeys" for him. I was led to believe that we could expect some kind of quid pro quo, although I didn't allow the conversation to get that far.

Over the weeks in camp, we find that the trails are pretty well marked, and our guides are helpful, leading us to viable habitats we can still catch on tape without too much outside noise coming from the camp or traffic several miles away. There remains the problem of stream noise, however, which affects the work.

At night, the rats run amok in our cabin. Since no one has figured out how to supply oxygen to the head-boxes we're supposed to use, we opt to sleep unprotected, and they occasionally run over our pillows. As in Karisoke, we reacclimate ourselves to them after a while. Last night, one creature ate through several layers of nylon backpack material, sealed thick plastic, and tin foil to reach my stash of granola. It left a huge hole in the side of the backpack, which I then spent the better part of a precious good-weather day (of course) repairing since it was my only available means of carrying equipment and supplies through the forest.

Tuesday, March 12th

0530 hours. We set up to record in a wonderful spot just before dawn today. Our guide, who we cannot seem to get rid of, is standing a hundred meters away, smoking and coughing incessantly. The mics we use are so sensitive, he can be heard a quarter of a mile away, flicking the flint wheel of his lighter, then snapping it shut. This happens every few minutes and is terribly annoying. Even though we've asked him to go back to camp and leave us, he hangs around. Shamas (songbirds) and gibbons begin to sing from a distance. But now there's traffic from three kilometers (nearly two miles) away. Exasperated, we return to camp at 0900 hours, eat breakfast, then prepare to return to the forest for midday and afternoon ambience. We try everything to get away from noise today, but the wind has shifted, and traffic from the road completely overwhelms us. We give up for the night and try to think of things to write in our diaries. Perhaps we can make up a good story or two.

Wednesday, March 13th

Much better! We get siamang (a type of gibbon) vocalizing this morning—and very close at that. We stand under a tree alongside the trail, and a couple of different animals let go with a marvelous chorus seemingly just for us. Also, we get an excellent dawn chorus, which makes up for yesterday. Ruth tries recording termites, but they're not vocal like their kin in Tanzania—at least not today. After breakfast, we hear that a sun bear (the smallest weighs in around a hundred pounds) and python (one of the largest) were sighted nearby, and we head out to investigate. By the time we arrive, they are long gone. But there are leeches everywhere. Usually, I set my Sony recorder, which is the size of a medium-sized book, on the ground. The machine is powered by a set of eight D-cell batteries, both of which get warm when the machine is recording. Leeches love heat, and if I'm not careful, the battery pack and recorder are literally covered with hundreds of undulating, inch-long creatures slithering over everything in my pack, including my water bottle and lunch.

By 1600 hours we have secured orang grunt vocalizations, leaf monkeys, and a Munkjak deer barking in the forest. This is the same location we recorded at earlier. It seems as if all the animals we had on our list today converged in this place for one rare performance. On our way back to camp this evening, millions of spiders on the forest floor reflect light coming from our head lamps off of the retinas of their eyes. Looks like the Los Angeles basin at night from high up on Mulholland Drive. When we shut down our headlamps, caterpillars, whose tails glow with two bright bioluminescent spots, take us completely by surprise. Also, the forest floor is lit with the bioluminescent glow of the abundant fungi. Between the sounds and available biological light, I am beginning to understand how hunter-gather groups might be able to safely navigate over great distances at night through this terrain without the aid of torches or other illumination.

The wind comes up at around 2000 hours. Just when we begin to feel safe, Ary warns us to watch out for falling trees. It's the greatest danger to people unfamiliar with the forest, he tells us. The fertile soil runs only a few inches in depth. The tree roots splay out over large distances and do not descend beyond the range of nutrients offered by the thin top layer. When the wind blows or rainwater coats their upper canopy, the trees become top-heavy and topple without warning. On our way back to camp, Ruth stumbles upon an eighteen-inch long, black-and-white pit viper. Ruth observes the creature in the beam of her flashlight and determines that, while quite dangerous, it is indifferent to us for now. She takes out her pocket flash camera and, bending quite close, clicks off several shots.

Saturday, March 16th. Bohorok in northern Sumatra

The site Ary has chosen to take us to is our greatest nightmare—a tourist camp. Neither of us can understand why he chose this spot, considering the conditions we placed on the trip while planning it with him in Jakarta. It is filled with several hundred families visiting for the weekend. Like all summer vacationers, these folks are celebrating. With guitars (amplified and otherwise), boomboxes, soccer games, music from the restaurant, and the playing at the nearby river, noise resonates everywhere. Ruth and I, limited by our time and energies, are quite baffled. There's an orang feeding station in a nearby forest above the camp where—I can only guess—Ary thought we would get some of the long calls high on our list of things to record. However, it's one of many tourist attractions, so thirty or forty people go at a time to visit the primates. Because of the way our trip is scheduled, we're trapped here for a few days with no transportation unless we want to hitchhike, which we don't, not with a couple of hundred pounds of technology. At times like this, I begin to despair and become very quiet.

Anticipating a rare chance to record tonight, I spend the day hiding in my cabin, trying to rest because the noise in camp kept me up all last night. Ruth has gone off to search for a quiet place. At lunch, in the dining room, I watch a young female cat sitting on my table, begging for scraps of food. As she rotates her ears independently in many different directions, I get an idea. With some paper, scotch tape, and nail polish, I fabricate a set of ears in the shape of the cat's and mount them, along with two small mics, onto either side of my earphones. When I switch on the recorder, the binaural effect is anything but subtle. It enhances the stereo space dramatically so that it sounds as one might hear normally—up, down, all around. Truly astounding! I can't get away from the noise tonight, but the sounds of bat fly-bys, insects, and birds moving around the space where I sit on the trail are enough to convince me that my new ears work rather well. Tomorrow we leave for Borneo, and I'll know for sure.

Wednesday, March 20th. Camp Leakey, Tanjung Puting, Kalimantan (Borneo)

Our dugout canoe is tethered to one of the million aerial roots that define a mangrove swamp, just a few kilometers from camp. We've paddled here very carefully since the waterline is inches from the gunwale and our canoe is loaded with valuable gear—never mind the crocs that line the shore of this black-water river. Tannin from the decaying vegetation turns the water a dark tea-like color. The water looks murky and dark, but is often quite drinkable if there aren't too many humans or domestic animals nearby. Recently, because a couple of Indonesian and German mining operations have set up camp upstream, mercury has been dumped into the river so we aren't inclined to taste the water on this trip. Problem with the color is that it's difficult to pick out objects more than an inch or so below the surface even though the river water might be otherwise quite clear.

With my new "ears," I'm trying to record afternoon ambience, so I'm not paying much attention. For a long while, other than the sounds of insects, birds, and distant proboscis monkeys, it's very quiet. After several minutes of recording, I hear a number of splashes coming from nearby. At first, they don't signal anything particular to me. Could be a fallen branch, a diving bird, or even a fish leaping out of the water to capture an insect.

I attach the "ear" system to a nearby tree to see if I could achieve the same effect as I had with the earphones on my head. It worked so well that my attention is completely drawn to the recording, and I neglect to notice what is going on around the boat until my eye catches an unusual disturbance on the water, inches away from where I am sitting. Then I see another ripple, followed by several more. When the scaled back of a croc breaks the nearby surface, I realize that we are surrounded by many more than I can accurately count.

While not particularly large by croc standards, the animals in this river have jaws which, nevertheless, can close around prey with a force approaching 5,000 pounds per square inch, enough to put a hole or two in my leg. Trying to remain cool under the circumstances, I remark in measured, even tones to Ruth, who is sitting in the bow, "I don't like this. I think we should probably go, *now*." It was one of the few times in my experience in the field with her that she didn't hang around to find out what would happen next.

Tuesday, March 26th. Tanjung Harapan, Borneo

This afternoon, on the way to Camp Leakey, we stop along the river to record proboscis monkeys but get caught in an approaching thunderstorm. Avoiding ground leeches trying to bore through our shoes, we huddle for shelter under the thatched roof of an abandoned hut. I set up my mics just in time to capture some of the loudest claps of thunder I've ever heard. This storm is dramatic and wonderful, echoing throughout the forest as the birds and insects sing along in the fading light of the day. All of our equipment is working, and we get remarkable material.

Gathering and showing more always and with velocity,

When I first began to write about sound and nature, I looked up the word nature in *Webster's Unabridged Dictionary of the English Language* (1972) just for fun. Here's what I found: "(a) nude; naked as one is when born; (b) uncivilized; (c) not cultivated or tamed; wild; savage; (d) unrenewed in spirit; unregenerate; at enmity with God." While this is what I had always understood before seeing and hearing nature for myself, it is quite different from the nature I have come to know. What is described as "naked," I find gloriously outfitted. What is noted as "uncivilized," I find elegantly refined. What is explained as "not cultivated," I find hopeful. And what is defined as being at "enmity with God," I find to be God's very essence. Once there, I discovered that, to me, every living thing in the natural world is both separate and different while, at the same time, absolutely dependent on all other forms of life; a composite where everything miraculously interacts and interrelates. I had to come to terms with the distances I felt when experiencing wilderness or wildness in the natural world by describing the encounter as a kind of ecotone. This is the place in the margins that Florence Krall speaks about in her book of the same name. In a footnote, she refers to Nature as meaning "the nonhuman as well as the human components of the Earth and the processes that bind organisms and nonliving environment in interrelationships." Nature and Earth are capitalized "to emphasize the specificity and numinous quality of this dwelling place and of life processes." For me, it also comprises an unquantifiable, primary experience of the natural world—something I've learned through many hours of listening to the sounds of many different habitats. I do not experience this forest music in a romantic sense, but rather, with a high level of acceptance that comes with the certainty that there are many permutations of environment. Therein lies the wonder for me.

I can't help but speculate why, in our culture, the word nature has such a strong context all its own. Significantly, in all of the approximately 300 Native American languages in North America, not one has a single word for nature or, for that matter, wilderness or wildness. The comparisons with our own language and words for the natural world continue to fascinate me and, at the same time, make me very suspicious of what we continue to do in relation to it.

For those reasons, the word nature is rarely used to describe my work except as a reference. At times, I admit, I am tempted because it would be so much easier to do so. Meanwhile, my culture continues to use the term even as it separates us from the wild natural by a substantial and growing margin. In this way, we maintain a sense of superiority instead of seeking balance, arrogance in lieu of humility.

I've never been able to describe much about the natural world through words. However, the solutions are easier for me when trying to convey aspects of the wild natural through sound. David Abram, in his book, *The Spell of the Sensuous* (Pantheon Books, 1996), suggests that we in Western culture do not possess the language to express the requisite connections to the wild natural and that we somehow need to recover that link through the introduction of new words. Of course, there are other handicaps, as well. The models of nature I have been taught are greatly distorted. Where I was once taught that I could understand the wild natural by examining a bird out of context of the forest where it lived, I've learned that the interrelated components of the forest are so vast that none of us can ever hope to know them all. The natural world holds secrets that it is very slow to reveal. But I am eager to learn and to share with others what I have come to know.

Infinite and omnigenous and the like of these among them;

As I listened long and hard enough, both with and without headphones on, I began to discern certain patterns of sound that had never been described before. In a kind of biophany, the moment when the natural world reveals a secret, I first experienced unique acoustic patterns while working in Africa in the early eighties. As a result, wherever I travel, I still try to make recordings of every site I visit. I have spent much of my life building a natural sound archive that represents entire habitats. To date, my library, The Wild Sanctuary Sound Archives, consists of about 3,500 hours of material—20 percent of it lamentably from now-extinct habitats. Instead of believing that fragile environments can be continuously and endlessly developed, people must begin to listen and observe what changes are taking place. The world of commerce (of which we are all a major part) thinks of the natural world as a resource: profits, yes; consequences, no. But the world has changed in ways we cannot even imagine. Economics plays a major role in this current mutation.

Some developmental advocates have suggested that if just small biological islands of primary growth habitats are preserved, that will be enough—especially for the development of eco-tourism. However, it has been shown in our own country, from work done in North American national parks, that many formerly abundant species are becoming extinct at an increasing rate and are doing so in an inverse relationship to the size and age of the parks. The smaller the park, the faster the decay. For example, when we have tried to record in new stands of trees planted in the Olympic peninsula by Georgia-Pacific and other lumber companies, we have found a surprising biophonic lack of relationship between vocal creatures, evidenced by a scarcity of clear graphic definition in our sonograms and, more so, by the deafening silence. This is probably due to the homogeneous corn-rowed stands of fast-growing conifers and lack of supporting vegetation growing on the forest floor, habitats that the normal mix of creatures have not repopulated. Compare these recordings with those of nearby, healthy old-growth forests, and the measurable differences are astounding. Yet we are continually reassured that the new growth is healthy. Whenever I hear this argument, I can't help thinking, again, that I'm that Lancashire coppy gasping for oxygen in a wire cage.

The niche hypothesis has only recently been considered a valuable tool for defining the health of habitats. Adding this information to the body of biological knowledge is important for many reasons, not the least of which is the rediscovery of a direct cultural link to our natural surroundings before they all disappear.

The unaltered biophony of our temperate, tropical, arctic, desert, and marine habitats is becoming exceedingly rare and difficult to find. We are just beginning to discover that the keys to our musical past and the origins of complex intraspecies connection are still found in the unbroken acoustic fabric of these wonderful places.

Not too exclusive toward the reachers of my remembrancers,

Essentially, the relationship of humans with the natural world and its wonders has a history of being adversarial and isolated. This is especially evident when we try to replicate aspects of the wild natural in our natural history museums and aquaria. In many of these spaces, animals are lumped together in contained areas: African species mixed with Asian, estuary with open ocean. The audio media used to reproduce this material is not much better. Frequently set up in reverberant or noisy outdoor spaces and competing with other events, the sound is often boring and hard to hear. Video material is also of poor quality. And many museums, zoos, and aquaria are still using antiquated push-a-button, hear-a-sound (or see-an-event) systems. For me as a visitor, nothing much is gained from these encounters, as they are so far from useful experience. As part of my own work, I have gone to lengths to address these problems through the development of new technologies that play back sound as it would be heard in a natural state. When these systems are used to play back excellent field recordings, the visitor is able to experience a bit of the wild. In doing so, we've begun to address the art of recreating natural environments more realistically. Other forms of sound art, however, still lag behind.

For instance, what has happened to Western musical expression and our so-called connection to the natural? Our art forms have become so detached from our direct experience with the wild that, while aspects of music attempt to emulate or express nature, none I've heard sounds particularly convincing. Some composers may take the melodious voice of a thrush or warbler and be inspired to write a symphony as a result. However, the articulation of the bird through the limits of Western instrumental voices, elaborate compositional techniques, or computers doesn't begin to capture the dramatic aural complexities and textures one experiences in natural habitats. Yet some of us still fool ourselves into thinking we are able to capture its essence. As Claude Lévi-Strauss wrote in his recent book, titled *Look, Listen, Read,* "an uninformed listener cannot say that it is the sea in Debussy's composition of the same name...but once the title is known, one visualized the sea on hearing...*La Mer.*"

I suspect that we are functionally incapable of reaching back far enough in time to be able to make the important distinctions between what we have composed or orchestrated and what really exists in the wilderness. Long ago, we acquired our musical heritage largely from the animal world, of which we were once a collective and integral part. We now earn our musical certification by degree at institutions like Juilliard, Eastman, the Paris Conservatory, Yale, or through a grant from the NEA. Having experienced more than a little of both worlds, it is my impression that modern music education does not appear to be linked in any way to the natural world. Roy Lichtenstein once said, "artists try to tell you that what they do comes from nature, and I'm always trying to tell you that what I do is completely abstract." To me, it is the sound from the unaltered natural world that is the real music I love most.

Paul Shepard, in his book, *The Others: How Animals Made Us Human* (Island Press, 1996), reminds us of the Greek tale of Orpheus, "who created music and taught it to the astonished beasts." He then goes on to say that the Greeks had it backwards. It was the animals who first made music, and it was our ancestors who listened. "When humans uttered their first words," he continues, "birds, frogs, and insects were already whistling, dancing, drumming, and trilling." One evening, while on a field trip to Africa commissioned by the California Academy of Sciences, I heard what I thought was a group of these amazing creatures chorusing in a kind of harmonious synchronicity—a cohesive and precise animal orchestration that was special to that particular habitat. This biophany was a revelation that began to challenge some tenaciously-held Eurocentric notions I had believed for so long.

In my own life, I have been recording natural sound and utilizing the results as components of orchestration since 1968, when I first began this odyssey. I love the task of recording and creating, and I can't imagine doing anything else more blessed in this life. I like to think of myself as a fairly competent naturalist, field recordist, and producer who, until very recently, spent an average of seven months a year in the field, often alone. I don't fear the natural world, its creatures, or the events I encounter. However, I have come to greatly respect it and have learned its dangers firsthand. Nevertheless, I feel much more comfortable and safe when I'm alone in a rainforest or a desert at night than I do when walking around the streets of Manhattan, Los Angeles, or Paris in broad daylight, or enduring the pitfalls of academia or the business world. The apparent contradiction here is that I prefer living in the presence of wildness, in the ecotone where *uncertainty* is the expectation. At least, there, the limits of uncertainty are knowable. Yet my Western conditioning is so strong that I am always reluctantly and sadly drawn back to the "civilized" world I have grown up knowing. Psychologically, I am unable to make the final break, so at best, my relationship with the wildness is more or less tenuous. At the same time, there is a kinship to the wild (perhaps genetic) that I cannot escape no matter how hard I try. And so I live in two worlds: romantically desiring to be in one (evidenced by my work), and inevitably being sucked back into the sullen realities of the other (also evidenced by my work).

One of the things I like best about wildness is the profound lack of judgment. A creature either thrives or it doesn't. I am either prey or a predator, and I have learned enough to distinguish between the two and to make certain choices about my behavior in the presence of the Others. Without a serious weapon, I become simply one of the many— certainly more equal—and the experience has taught me a kind of humility that I was quite unlikely to learn living primarily in cities, the rural countryside, or at any university. Ego counts for zip in the bush.

As a recordist, though, I am a voyeur, taking what I can for the moment within the limitations of my equipment. I used to think that what I captured on tape was "authentic." I know better, now, and have become much more modest with my claims. The abstractions I capture with current technologies, be they music or ambience, are nothing more than a mere shadow, much like the phantoms that once played out their hour on Plato's cave wall—a kind of delusion, a speculation void of context and meaning that is further distorted as we confine those iterations to compact discs. I realize that the very act of recording these habitats means to dissect the natural—carefully selecting for time, place, dynamic creature performance—then further choosing one small aspect to create new contexts akin to an ideal expression of whatever aural vision momentarily comes to mind. I've traveled long distances to collect what John Cage somewhat disparagingly referred to as "found compositions." Like most of us, he missed the point. But, there still remains a viable context where human-created music is directly connected *with* "nature." In some of the few forest-dwelling groups of people whose music, stories, and culture still resonates with birdsong and the throbbing choruses of frogs at dawn or dusk, the tenuous synapse remains.

Shortly after my 1983 trip to Kenya, where I first considered the niche hypothesis, I had an opportunity to visit both Australia and southern Ecuador, where I encountered the Pitjantjara and Jivaro groups, respectively. The Pitjantjara of central Australia move through what, to us, may look like completely flat and undifferentiated terrain. To them, however, it is described to a significant degree by sound definitions of their ancient routes (songlines): "Travel along this route as long as you hear the green ants sing, then, when their song ends, head toward another voice (and so on) until you get to your destination."

The Jivaro were former headhunters who continued to rearrange the skull sizes of their adversaries until the late sixties. In 1599, after wiping out a Spanish-controlled town of around 20,000 inhabitants, they were considered to be so fierce that they earned a reputation as the only South American tribe to effectively repel these Iberian invaders. On one visit, when I was allowed to accompany a group of men on a night hunt, I was astounded to discover that they found their way through the densest foliage without the aid of torches, guided primarily by subtle changes in forest sounds. With amazing accuracy, they were able to describe unseen animals far down the path by the slightest variation of insect and frog articulation. Their music, too, seemed to reflect a notable relationship to the sounds around them and often appeared to be driven by the "mood" of the forest daytime or evening sounds.

Unfortunately, I was too focused on separating human sounds from those of the forest at that time and did not think to record the music and forest ambience together. So I was able to capture the forest on tape and left behind one of the more relevant links in a fit of ignorance. I deeply regret this oversight but honestly didn't know better. Other discoveries, however, are beginning to reveal new evidence of links we have long dispensed with in our own culture.

There has been a great deal of work done recently by people like Louis Sarno, who has been living with the Babenzélé (Bayaka) Pygmies in the rainforests of the Central African Republic. Sarno suggests that music and language of the Bayaka arises from the biophony of their respective environments, among many other influences. The relationship between the music of the Bayaka and sounds of the forest seems so strong that they often appear to use the environmental sounds as a kind of natural karaoke orchestra to which they perform. He adds that one of the most robust links is an association to the forest and its creature voices that is strongly spiritual and social, where their music becomes at once both a replication and reflection. Other anthropologists suggest that it is too simplistic to offer that music and language are *directly* influenced by the sounds of the forest. That may be. However, Sarno and both I feel that there may be some areas that have previously been overlooked *precisely* because they are so elusive and difficult to quantify.

In Sarno's book/compact disc, *Bayaka: the Extraordinary Music of the Babenzélé Pygmies* (Ellipsis Arts, 1995), sounds of the forest can be heard mixed with the music in a representative way. After I finished the production, samples were sent to Sarno to play for the Bayaka singers and instrumentalists. They were asked to pay special attention to the relationship between the ambient sounds and music. With the exception of a comment about the shortness of a particular "Boyobi" performance (a ceremony which is normally performed over a period of many hours or even days) the work was universally accepted by those who created it.

There are, of course, other models of this interdependent phenomenon of natural sound directly influencing music. Some Native American music of North, Central, and South America, for instance, is still joined to its respective environment in ways more or less similar to that of the Bayaka. However, this marvel is disappearing at a rate linked to that of habitat destruction combined with the impact of Western religious missions. Luther Standing Bear (1868–1939) expressed this forcefully: "Only to the white man was the natural world a 'wilderness' and only to him was the land 'infested' with 'wild' animals and 'savage' people. To us it was tame. Earth was bountiful, and we were surrounded with the blessings of the Great Mystery. Not until the hairy man from the east came and with brutal frenzy heaped injustices upon us and the families we loved was it 'wild' for us. When the very animals of the forest began fleeing from his approach, then it was that for us the 'Wild West' began."

The missionaries were very late in realizing that the souls of the Yup'ik (Eskimos) in Eek, Alaska, were worth saving in 1920. Mostly, there was a scarcity of valuable economic resources in the remote territories of southwestern Alaska. Fur seals were some distance away, and other fur-bearing animals were not as plentiful as in other areas. Gold was nowhere nearby, and fish, moose, and bear, their staples for food, clothing, and shelter, were not terribly useful on the open market. However, when the "robed ones" finally arrived just after World War I, bans were immediately imposed on "pagan" ritual music and dance, forcing it immediately underground for over half a century. Fortunately, Chuna McIntyre's grandmother survived well into her nineties and passed on to him a wonderful legacy of traditional song, dance, ritual, and prayer that he has recreated in his album, *Drums Across the Tundra,* which I produced in 1993. The reverential expressions of the natural world and animal references in this tape are remarkable, and the material is currently being reintroduced into the tribal ceremonies and culture. Finally, after seventy years, this rich heritage of music from the wild is reluctantly tolerated by resident churches.

When the question is readdressed, "What does either the Bayaka, the Pitjanjara, the Jivaro, and some Native American music have to do *with* 'nature?'" a different answer begins to emerge. In most instances, to me, the relationship is palpable if not directly correlated. However, where it still exists, it is because the point at which the two elements merge is seamless. There is no conflict. No contradiction. It is bonded to the lives of these humans in fundamental ways I can only dream about for ourselves.

The natural world will reveal its mysteries to us when we begin to think of ourselves as an integral part of the whole—when we think of it not simply as an economic resource but as a font of spiritual renewal. Westerners, in our daily rush to reinvent or validate ourselves, haven't given much time to this consideration. Consequently we, as a culture, no longer have any close spiritual ties to the natural world. From the changes in myself during the course of my work, it has become clear that this nexus is a fundamental ingredient we will have to learn to accept once again. In addition, to comprehend the relevance of birdsong, we must come to know the voices of insects, frogs, and mammals vocalizing at the same time and learn the myriad complex ways in which they all relate to one another. Otherwise, the "facts" we have learned will not necessarily provide the insights we need.

We can no longer separate creatures from the complex structure where they live and vocalize in and hope to learn very much about them. And for true spiritual renewal, we need to give ourselves time in the wild. A week or ten days in the field won't suffice because time in the forest is necessarily experienced differently. A digital wristwatch beeping off the hours has no relevance. Animals don't meet at any fixed hour to sleep, forage, or hunt. Instead, intervals are determined by the cycles of seasons, the right amount of morning light to trigger birds and insects into song, the passing cells of weather, the dappled shadings of light on the forest floor as the day progresses, and the distinct fragrances that arise at various parts of day or night. Of course, true wildness manages to evade capture on audio tape, film, or any other medium. They simply cannot be *explained*. After being present below the canopy of an equatorial rainforest for a very long time, the tactile, aural, and visual constituents eventually unite, and the creature voices become both unified and distinctive. Only at that point do I begin to hear tiny fragments of what might possibly inspire the hunter-gatherers who live nearby to begin an ancient chant. The forest becomes my place of worship, and my mind begins to imagine what it must have been like to be part of that creature world we have so long ago forsaken and devalued. How would our music sound if, given all the wonderful experience and technologies we possess, we could only find a way to reconnect once again with the Others for one brief moment?

I cannot presently see Western music, or for that matter, any art form, as being linked *with* "nature." It is the intricate and resonant music of the Bayaka, the Jivaro, the Kaluli, or the Yup'ik Eskimos that I long to hear over and over again, precisely because it springs from the sounds of natural environments and is not yet severed from its origins. When I wish to hear the voice of a bird, or a wolf, or a whale, I'll take the time to visit where it lives. At the same time, I'll listen hard for the songs of neighboring humans whose lives are intimately bound to that which sustains them. I'm willing to take the risk that these performances just might occur in ways I'm unlikely to hear in an urban concert hall or on a well-packaged compact disc.

Only much later in my life, after many reinventions of myself and when I was well into middle-age, did I realize that the sounds of the natural world created a robust music of their own—one that I would come to love and would come to use as a palette for my sound sculptures and musical orchestrations. Often, when I can do nothing to improve on the raw field recordings, I sit alone and play them softly, trying to imagine the enchanted moment of their creation. When I'm in a creative state, I'm in a no-man's land between life and death. We all find our own path whether it be toward our own voice or tethered to that of an Other. Sometimes it's a combination of both. Either way, I make the choice to leap into the unknown.

Picking out here one that I love,

I learned to listen by sitting quietly for long periods of time in natural, quiet places and trying to hear as non-humans might. To do this, I have built extensions to my ears out of paper and scotch tape and tried to use them as a cat might—first focusing both in one direction, then another, then turning each one in different directions. To hear worms moving under the surface of the soil, I placed a hydrophone (underwater microphone) on the surface of the ground where a robin had been focusing its attention just moments before. To hear sand dunes sing, I have stood at the crest of the Kelso Dunes in the Mojave on Kelbaker Road, just north of Interstate 40. These are some of the actions that have changed my life and guide the ways in which I choose to enjoy each day. However, it hasn't freed me from resistance from some colleagues and peers.

Because I know that most of us are confused about what we experience and how to portray what we think we see or hear, I'm usually not bothered by such criticism. But there are times. One day, after making a presentation on the subject of natural sound, I played some music I had composed entirely with animal voices. Because this was largely an academic audience, several folks were outraged by the process and the result. "You're doing violence to animals!" said John Cage, the late composer, writer, and artist. "And you've changed their sound," added one of his colleagues. Feeling like some kind of biological felon, I waited until all the criticisms were expressed, most of which had to do with changing the sound so radically.

"First of all," I pointed out, "most of the sounds weren't changed. It's just that none of you sitting here have moved far enough away from your insular environments to really hear what's out there in the forest or below the surface of the water near a coral reef." Fully prepared for this response, I pressed on, saying that no recording represents an "authentic" sound any more than an Ansel Adams photograph of "Half Dome" *is* Half Dome, or a Marty Stouffer wildlife film with a predator-prey scene happens as he contends.

In my field, every microphone, every cable through which the electrical impulses travel, every component of every recorder, digital or otherwise, is calibrated with enough difference to create a distinctive variance between discrete recorded representations of the same material. Each type of microphone, for instance, gathers sound in a specific kind of pattern. Some mics, called omnis, pick up sound with equal sensitivity coming from all directions. A shotgun mic, on the other hand, picks up sound coming from a very narrow pattern based on the direction it is pointed, tending to eliminate most other audio information. There are many kinds of patterned mics in between those extremes, as well as different ways in which mics are powered to receive sound.

Most importantly, a sound, once recorded in the field and then brought into the studio, is completely out of context. Typically, sound is presented in stereo. Coming out of only two speakers, it is reduced once again to a narrower field. So in order to create the illusions of depth and moment, there needs to be a great deal of processing, mixing, and editing to make the sounds translate from one medium (the natural world) to another (artificial spaces). The birdsong is not *exactly* the bird. Aesthetically, it is a poor representation and not nearly as exciting as when it's heard in the context of the forest along with the tactile and visual cues. The elaborate equipment we humans have developed is often regarded by us as being omnipotent and without fault. But, at best, it is limited and replicates our world poorly and in far fewer dimensions than we have been conned into believing.

Furthermore, with our world turned upside down, we have learned to hear mostly what we see. Standing by the seashore, we gaze at the water lapping at our feet; it is only then, as we concentrate on the image, that we hear the tiny bubbles in the sand fizzle all around us. Our attention then shifts to the breakers thirty of forty yards offshore as they surge, curl, and crash. We no longer hear the bubbles, as our attention has shifted. Then, as we peer down the beach at the breakers, we hear the low roar of many waves and are almost totally unaware of the sounds just inches away from our ears. One cannot go the ocean shore, set up a microphone, and hope to record waves. The technology simply won't allow a successful replication of the sound. To accomplish the illusion, an audio naturalist must combine recordings of near-field, mid-field, and far-field elements just to begin to approach the experience of being at the shore. Gregory Bateson once observed, "The map is not the territory." Nor do the utterances we hear on tape represent the biophony of the forest. It's simply impossible to capture God's choir in a recording.

Choosing to go with him on brotherly terms.

Recently, I was invited to speak at a museum of wildlife art in a very well-heeled community located in the West. A spectacular and expensive new building, it featured the work of contemporary artists, photographers, and sculptors, mostly from the "realist" school. When I entered the facility for the first time, I was struck by the hushed silence as images of wildlife were represented in every still visual form.

During the afternoon, as I was setting up my sound system in the auditorium, the curator came by and introduced herself, asking what I did. I told her that I produce sound sculptures for museums and public spaces (hoping to pique her interest in possibly inviting us to create a work of art). Impatiently, she snapped back, "I have no idea what you're talking about. I haven't got a lot of time because I'm very busy. *What* is a sound sculpture?"

Thrown off guard by her attitude, I tried to collect myself and told her that like the visual world, with sound sculptures, we take the sound medium and sculpt it much as artists do in any "hard" form (clay, metal, ceramic). The results, when commissioned to the fullest extent of our technical and production capabilities, are three-dimensional biophonies that fill anything from small spaces to whole large rooms. Expressed in the pieces are textures of a place, feelings of light and dark, negative and positive spaces, kinetics, color, form, tension and release, and, of course, content representing location, environment, and time of day. Additionally, the pieces provide visitors with experiences and transport them to places in ways impossible through the application of other media.

"You've lost me completely," she said. "I simply don't understand."

Trying another angle, I said, "We try to bring life to spaces by creating non-repeating audio environments that evoke a sense of place in ways not possible with visual elements. How else can you portray wind, or the dynamics of a rainstorm, or the thunder of ocean waves, or the motion of a hawk circling overhead?"

I could see from her expression and body language, that I wasn't getting through. She slowly edged away from me toward the door as if I were a deranged wild creature. My hope for casting a wider net in this wonderful art space was falling on deaf ears.

"Why don't you come to my presentation tonight and you'll hear what I'm driving at," I said. "I'm introducing some special new material: ants singing, trees drumming..."

"I can't," she interrupted, glancing at her watch. "I have a four-year-old, and I have to babysit tonight. And anyway, my child *hates* ants!"

In a final controlled cry of anguish and on the verge of hysteria, she gave it one last try. "I don't understand what you are trying to accomplish. What do you *see*?" she said.

Completely exhausted, the only answer I could think of was, "Nothing." I took a deep breath, remembering the silent, dead pictures hanging on the wall, and thought, "Thank God."

For me, hearing the natural world as a biophonic orchestra has brought a measure of delight into my life. As the canary needs fresh air, I thrive with natural sound and have been gratified by its presence. I haven't yet got to the point where I am looking back, spending my days and nights listening to recordings of places I have lived and worked. That time will come soon enough. But when I am in the middle of a production for a museum or aquarium, and I put on a recording to create a piece for visitors to enjoy, I often get carried away, listening and remembering how this or that environment once was and how, sadly, in my lifetime, most no longer are. Listening to those moments brings an enormous sense of pleasure to me, which is why I continue to create these offerings in their several forms of sound art on compact disc and in public spaces.

—

"What is essential, is invisible to the eye." St. Exupery's aphorism expresses most everything I feel and have come to know. It has been my experience that the truths imposed are not always the truths revealed, something my grandmother tried to teach me. She was an immigrant with the equivalent of an eighth grade education who spoke four languages and read everything she could get her hands on. It was no accident that she happened to know something about the classics and philosophy, both of which we'd discuss when I visited her during the late fifties. "I don't know what they're teaching you in college, but from what you're telling me, I think it's *dreck*! Plato was a schmuck, a real wise-guy always trying to convince people he *knew* something about truth. I'll take Socrates any day. Now there was a *mensch*. They killed him, you know. Destroyed all his writings. And do you know what those bastards accused him of? They accused him of asking the question, 'why?' Now *there's* a dangerous thing to do, *boychick*. Remember," she said, "no institution wants to be asked why it's doing something. But if you want to get to the truth, keep asking."

Biophonies

Aberdare Salient, Kenya

I have forgotten how quickly the sun rises and sets at the equator. In a fleeting moment, our campsite is light or dark and the biophony changes. We have arrived just before the rains come, and it is a time when all of the thirsty animals congregate tightly around the few available depressions of available water. The drama of competition for accessible space, food, and water is fierce this evening. Now, at sundown, a family of giant forest pigs comes into view near where I am set up to record. The ferocious roars of the alpha male create a tension felt by every nearby creature, expressed by the frantic calls and desperate wing beats of Egyptian geese and other birds as they make quickly make their exit. The colobus monkey's soft, low, ratchet-like, pulsing voice offers a soothing respite in-between the bellows of the pigs, who seem determined to stake their claim to the muddy banks.

Trout Lake, Washington. Dawn

The nearest road is seven miles to the west in a straight line, yet we clearly hear the sound of trucks and cars over the din of the spring chorus taking place here. Even though our location is so remote, it's been difficult to find a time to record when there's no human sound. This morning, we're in luck; it rained last night so the spring air is clear and cool, and a gentle wind from the east sends unwanted noises in another direction. Sounds of the riparian habitat around the lake are crisp and detailed. Humidity and the dew on the surrounding vegetation add reverberation to the biophonic performance. The early morning animal orchestra is enhanced by the echoing voice of a lone raven, circling high overhead, as mist lifts from the surface of the lake revealing a pair of loons, an osprey diving for breakfast, and many other waterfowl.

Mata Atlantica, Brazil. The Atlantic Rainforest

Tonight we are sitting in a dry rainforest. Less than 1 percent of this vibrant, original habitat is left, and, we are told by the resident biologist, it is unlikely to recover even if more land is made available. The creatures, human and Other, that once established the fragile balance in this space have been destroyed or displaced. We recorded woolly spider monkeys this afternoon and howlers this morning. My colleague, Ruth, is ecstatic—at the same time we are saddened to see the incredible devastation nearly everywhere we walk. It is never completely out of sight.

Rio de Janiero

We were invited to have dinner tonight with Antonio Carlos Jobim (composer of "Girl from Ipanema"). Throughout the meal, he recounts moments during his childhood when magical forests came right up to the edge of Rio, and he and his friends would play in the jungle performing with the animals. When we aren't talking, he imitates the calls and songs of the birds, frogs, and mammals he remembers—many now extinct—as if the vocalizations were in his native language. His poignant imitation of the passerine (finch) is particularly lovely. It is close to sunrise when we get back to our hotel. With no time for showers, we rush to the airport to catch a plane for the Amazon where we will record for many weeks.

Foothills of Mt. Lassen, California. 8 P.M.

I'll never forget the time a film company in Hollywood hired me to go to Iowa one August to record corn growing. I sat in the middle of a field all night long with my microphone held up to a stalk of corn waiting for some kind of sound—I had no idea what. As I waited, with mosquitoes having drawn every drop of available blood from my unprotected body, I found myself nodding off to the hypnotic evening rhythms of crickets and the occasional vocalization of a bullfrog from a nearby moonlit pond. Tonight is the closest I've come to that same epiphany since that magical evening song in Iowa years ago. (By the way, corn *does* make a sound as it grows telescopically. The rhythm can be quite close to the percussive break of a jazz drummer.)

Big Sur coast. Winter equinox

Today's my lucky day. Maybe it's because I'm with Katherine, my lover, my friend and, I'm hoping, my wife. I have tried for a dozen years or so to capture the feeling of ocean surf on tape so that the sound we hear over two speakers recreates the illusion we experience at the beach. This afternoon, I finally get it. The sounds have to be recorded in different stages, in much the same way that we sense the surge of waves with our eyes, on the surface of our skin, and with our sense of smell—all at once. What our eyes see, we're fooled into hearing. And so, with other sensations missing, the sounds alone need to be layered and textured to make up for our inability to hear.

Gray's Lake. Southeastern Idaho

After following us for many days now, the *National Geographic* camera crew finished shooting late today near a site where many sandhill cranes are nesting. This evening, I finally have a chance to camp alone in the mountains to the east and above the lake in the Caribous. The mosquitoes are particularly brutal, and I set my mics some distance from the tent to avoid recording the constant scratching of my numerous bites. With my earphones tight to my head, I lie back and know that soon the sonorous mixture of spring songbirds and insects at sundown will lull me into restful sleep. Tonight, I think back to my twenties, a time when I marked goals by trying to outrace the moment and get to the next event, whatever it was. If nothing was happening, I invented something or initiated it just to have the *feeling* that I was in motion. This was the result of never being at home spiritually or physically within myself. Life was experienced episodically—much like the telling of the early details of this story. That illusion evaporated the moment the decision was made to live more like the animal creature I am—in the instant of experience—alive, present, sentient, aware, unseparated from the abundance of life around me.

Amazon. Km41

As we were recording in the jungle tonight, we became aware of the unmistakable scent of a nearby jaguar. Ruth and I were alone in the forest, several kilometers from camp with no moon or other light apart from the beams from our flashlights. We never saw or heard the animal but knew it was nearby, perhaps only a few feet away. Our senses were certainly *heightened*, but I don't believe that either of us felt particularly afraid or sensed that we were in immediate danger. Sitting quietly about fifty meters apart, we recorded for an hour. The musky odor was always present—at times a bit stronger than others. Around midnight, Ruth and I went down the trail in different directions to try to collect the greatest variety of night sounds that we could in this wonderfully rich environment.

After fifteen minutes of walking, I sat down alone beside the trail and began to record. Only then did I hear the cat's low growl in my headphones. It must have been following me, but nothing I heard before the growl suggested it had come that close. The sound of the jaguar's breath in my earphones indicated that the cat was probably not more than an arms length from the mics I had set up just thirty feet down the trail. My heart was pounding so loud that I thought the sound, alone, would startle the animal. But I remained very still, clutching my recorder with a grip not usually recommended for extremely sensitive equipment. The intensity of the low growls and breaths from the creature indicated that it was sniffing the mics, although I couldn't see what was happening in the dark and had no intention of spooking it with my flashlight. An event that lasted no more than a minute seemed like a couple of hours as I sat there mesmerized by the power of the animal's voice, its breath, and the sounds of rumbles in its stomach.

Then, just as it appeared, the cat moved silently off into the forest, leaving behind the sounds of the throbbing pulses of frogs, a heart in a human body, and insects in the night. The jaguar is the strongest animal in this forest. A quarter the size of a full-grown horse, it could drag an animal that size and weight several miles through the forest with relative ease. Tonight, we have a natural relationship to each other—predator and prey—and for the moment we're respectful equals.

I returned to camp about an hour ago (3:00 A.M.), and I still can't sleep. Although I'm dead tired—Ruth and I got up to record the dawn chorus twenty-four hours ago, as we do most days in the field—I can't take in enough of the incredible sound this forest performs for me every minute. There is such precision and richness in the insect and frog orchestration, such a tight fit of creature voice harmonies. The howler monkeys, in particular, join the chorus with a deep-throated roar that can be heard for miles throughout the canopy. There is a sense of grace and continuity here that is deeply felt and which becomes more resonant with each breath I take. The unity of all these creatures overwhelms me as I become one with them, and my eyes well with tears. I feel blessed and lucky; at the same time I realize that most people will never know for themselves what I feel this night. I suspect that when we finally cast the creature world in a less evil and adversarial role, embracing it for its will to live, the human spirit, too, may begin to heal.

Acknowledgments

Paul Shepard suggests in the preface to his seminal book, *Nature and Madness*, that his work was filled with speculation. So is mine. Some of it comes from trying to reconstruct, from memory, aspects of history and influences in my life that have made a difference. The rest has to do with what I've been able to recover and learn from my contact with both the human and non-human worlds. Like Shepard, who does not apologize for his suppositions, neither do I. In his introduction, he speaks of wisdom: "the most mature expression of which is the capacity to gently bring others forward to it, as far as they are capable." Problem is, since the wisdom he speaks of—that which emanates from intimate contact with the wild natural—is not valued in our culture, there may be very little to bring us to. In my experience, there is not much left of the natural world. And the effect on all of us, particularly those living in North America, is staggering. The perspective that the natural world is a reserve of resources, primarily available to meet the material needs of our society, continually erodes an essential sense of being, thereby keeping the human psyche and spirit off-balance, afraid, angry, depressed, and defensive. One example is the insidious amassing of deadly weapons in more than half the homes in the United States, which seems to be proportional to the destruction of our remaining wild habitat. The irony is that by the time our natural world is depleted in the near future, there will not be much left to defend.

There are, however, some new paradigms to be considered, so perhaps it is not too late. Only recently, in the last forty years, have ideas resurfaced or emerged that have made a difference to me insofar as they confirm the value of what I have experienced in the field. The expression of these ideas has given me both the confidence to express what I have come to know and offered some impetus for hope. To these mentors, Loren Eiseley, Paul Shepard, Jack Turner, Florence Rose Shepard, Wallace Stegner, Aldo Leopold, and Ken Norris, I am grateful beyond my ability to respond in either spirit or kind.

To Malcolm Margolin, publisher of one of the more remarkable bodies of literature, my gratitude for his abundant faith in this project and for questioning every assertion. And to Julianna Fleming, whose diligence brought the art of the Edit to new levels and who added special life to the text, I am thankful beyond measure.

To my wife, lover, confidant, and soulmate, Katherine, no words can express the appreciation I feel for her help and encouragement at the worst and best of times, of which both were many.

Bernie Krause
Glen Ellen, California
May 1998

Discography

1. Nonesuch Guide to Electronic Music★	Nonesuch 1968
2. Ragnarök (w/Paul Beaver)	Limelite 1969
3. In a Wild Sanctuary (w/Paul Beaver)	Warner Brothers 1969
4. Gandharva (w/Paul Beaver)	Warner Brothers 1971
5. All Good Men (w/Paul Beaver)	Warner Brothers 1973
6. Citadels of Mystery	Takoma/Mobile Fidelity 1979
7. Revised Nonesuch Guide to Electronic Music★	Nonesuch 1979
8. Equator	Nature Co. 1986
9. Nature	Nature Co. 1987
10. Distant Thunder	Nature Co. 1988
11. Mountain Stream	Nature Co. 1988
12. Gentle Ocean	Nature Co. 1988
13. Jungle Shoes/Fish Wrap	Rykodisk 1988
14. Morning Song Birds	Nature Co. 1988
15. Sounds of a Summer's Evening	Nature Co. 1988
16. Tropical Rainforest	Nature Co. 1989
17. Gorilla	Nature Co. 1989
18. Gorillas in the Mix	Rykodisk 1989
19. Natural Voices/African Song Cycle	Wild Sanctuary 1990
20. Woodland Journey	Wild Sanctuary 1990
21. Meridian	Nature Co. 1990

22. Nez Perce Stories	Wild Sanctuary Word & Music	1991
23. Music of the Nez Perce	Wild Sanctuary Word & Music	1991
24. Tropical Thunder	Wild Sanctuary	1991
25. Wild Times at the Waterhole		
	Wild Sanctuary Creatures 'n' Kids™	1991
26. Drums Across the Tundra	Wild Sanctuary Word & Music	1992
27. Ishi, the Last Yahi	Wild Sanctuary Word & Music	1992
28. Discover the Wonder (Grades 3–6)	Scott Foresman	1992
29. Mata Atlantica (Atlantic Rainforest w/Ruth Happel)		
	Wild Sanctuary	1994
30-32. Nature's Lullabies (Wee Creatures Ages 1–3)		
Ocean/Rain/Stream	Wild Sanctuary	1994
33. African Adventures	Wild Sanctuary	1994
34. Bayaka: The Extraordinary Music of the Babenzélé Pygmies★★		
(Louis Sarno)	Ellipsis Arts	1995
35. Green Meadow Stream	Miramar	1998
36. Dawn at Trout Lake	Miramar	1998
37. Amazon Days, Amazon Nights	Miramar	1998
38. Ocean Wonders	Miramar	1998
39. Loons of Echo Pond★★ (Ruth Happel)	Miramar	1998
40. Desert Solitudes (w/Ruth Happel)	Miramar	1998
41. Ocean Dreams	Miramar	1998
42. Midsummer Nights (w/Ruth Happel)	Miramar	1998
43. A Wild Christmas (w/Phil Aaberg)	Miramar	1998
44. Whales, Wolves & Eagles of Glacier Bay	Miramar	1998
45. Rhythms of Africa (w/Rodney Franklin)	Miramar	1998
46. Rainforest Dreams (w/Rodney Franklin)	Miramar	1998
47. Ocean Odyssey (w/Rodney Franklin)	Miramar	1998
48. Borneo: Paradise in Kalimantan	Miramar	1998
49. Kalimantan: Heaven Before Time	Miramar	1998
50. Madagascar: The Fragile Land (w/Doug Quin)	Miramar	1998
51. Zimbabwe: Nature's Garden	Miramar	1998
52. Antarctica (w/Doug Quin)	Miramar	1998

★Standard Reference   ★★Executive Producer

BERNIE KRAUSE currently records the sounds of the natural wild with his company, Wild Sanctuary. He lives in Glen Ellen, California, with his wife, Katherine. He is also the author of *Notes From the Wild* (Ellipsis Arts, 1996).

JACK TURNER is the author of *The Abstract Wild* (University of Arizona Press, 1996).

— —

WILD SANCTUARY is an internationally known resource for natural sound and media design for public spaces featuring science and the arts. With one of the largest and most comprehensive private digital audio libraries, its mission is to provide natural sound and cultural renderings for museums, aquaria, zoos, and other large public environments, as well as an extensive line of premium quality audio CDs highlighting rare or extinct habitats throughout the world.

The Miramar nature recordings of Wild Sanctuary are available from record, book, and gift stores nationwide, as well as directly from Wild Sanctuary:

WILD SANCTUARY
(707) 996-6677; (707) 996-0280 fax
email: chirp@wildsanctuary.com
www.wildsanctuary.com

HEYDAY BOOKS publishes high quality books on California history, literature, natural history, and culture. For a free catalog, please contact:

HEYDAY BOOKS
P.O. Box 9145, Berkeley, CA 94709
(510) 549-3564; (510) 549-1889 fax
email: heyday@heydaybooks.com